Praise for *Acting is Your Business*

"Aspiring actors will benefit tremendously from the real-world practical advice provided by Wendy Kurtzman. As a well-respected casting director with a big picture understanding of both the actor's creative process and the nuts and bolts of the entertainment industry, she offers a holistic approach to an acting career—supporting creative passion with day-to-day achievable goals. Wendy connects the dots between artistic dreams and pragmatic results with a plan that will no doubt empower actors and hopefully guide them to fulfilment and success."

David Rubin, Emmy and Artios Award Winning Casting Director, Former President of the Academy of Motion Pictures Arts and Sciences

"*Acting is Your Business: How to Take Charge of Your Creative Career* provides a strategic formula for creating and sustaining a robust creative career while also offering tools for self care. When we launched the Pace University LA intensive for our BFA actors it was Wendy's knowledge and professional connections that elevated this program and cemented it as a truly unique and one-of-a-kind experience. Wendy's experience as a casting director and leader in the casting community makes her a great professor and mentor to our students."

Grant Kretchik, Head of BFA Acting, Chair of BFA Acting and BFA Film, TV, Voice Over, and Commercials, Sands College of Performing Arts, Pace University, USA

"Untold numbers of young people dream of becoming actors. Many invest good money in learning their craft. But few, if any, know how to navigate the industry once they complete their studies. Now they have a means to do so. Wendy Kurtzman's book provides a guide to aspiring actors to take charge of their own careers rather than waiting for others to deem them worthy. Having worked with Wendy as the casting director on many films I have seen her intelligence, impeccable taste, and love and respect for actors. Her years in the business have given her an intimate understanding of how it works. It is a thrill to see her willingness to share her knowledge with the next generation of artists. Wendy's book, and its easily accessible insights, is an invaluable asset to any actor interested in shortening the route from aspirant to fully engaged professional."

Harry Winer, Film and Television Director/Producer/Screenwriter, and Associate Professor, Kanbar Institute of Film & Television, New York University Tisch School of the Arts, USA

"Wendy Kurtzman has developed a university program that is one of the few if only classes that prepare young actors for the real world once they graduate from school. Her background enables her to not only discover talent but guide them through the mystery of the business that school does not provide them for. The students who take her class have a knowledge that most others do not."

Iris Grossman, Talent Manager, Echo Lake Entertainment, Former SVP of Talent and Casting at Turner Network Television (TNT)

"Wendy makes it her mission to obtain and provide all the necessary information that young actors need to transition from school into the industry. Her dedication to student development and her creation of the Pace Performing Arts intersession in LA is essential for our actors. They are transformed by their time with her. Our actors have a stronger sense of who they are as artists, gain knowledge of the aspects of the industry that they have control over, and they emerge from her sessions with a clear game plan. An actor that works with Wendy knows exactly what they need to do to show up prepared and confident."

Jennifer M. Holmes, Executive Director, Sands College of Performing Arts, Pace University, USA

"If you are an actor who wishes to be in control of your career and to put yourself in a position to succeed, then this is the book for you. Wendy Kurtzman provides a clear, manageable day-to-day, week-to-week, and year-to-year plan for the actor to plot their own unique career path. I celebrate this book for my students!"

John B. Benitz, Professor, Program Director BFA Screen Acting, Chapman University, USA

"Wendy is not only a colleague and a friend, she is also a respected and passionate casting professional. She has created a bridge for emerging artists to navigate the journey between academia and the entertainment business. This book is easy to read, proactive and empowering. A must have for any artist looking to sustain a creative career."

Leslie Litt, Emmy Nominated Casting Director and Senior Casting Executive, Freevee, Amazon Studios, *Friends*, *The Goldbergs*

"I have known Wendy Kurtzman as a casting director, a teacher and most importantly a mentor! She has shared her years of experience in the entertainment industry with young actors and has helped them navigate in a very tough industry. She takes so much pleasure in helping others and as an agent, I have always been so grateful for her knowledge and kindness."

Ro Diamond, Partner and Agent, SDB Partners, Inc.

"Wendy Kurtzman has had an amazing career as both a casting director and a professor but more importantly her inside knowledge and passion to share that is endless. I have known Wendy for a long time but to see her interact with her students is magic. Her thoughtfulness and knowledge she brings to the classroom are unmatchable."

Seth Yanklewitz, Artios Award Winning Casting Director, Former EVP of Talent and Casting at MGM, *The Hangover, New Girl, How I Met Your Father*

"This is the first book I have seen that helps the college graduate or acting workshop graduate navigate a career that uses the template of a successful business to make headway in a challenging career. As a professional casting director, Wendy has real life insight into the 'secret' of how actors get hired. As a college professor she has experience with what academia has to offer and where they failed with continued career guidance. There is a great need for the insightful, honest, and brilliant approach that Wendy guides the actor through with this book. Every actor who wants to work at their craft should take the time to read and practice the concepts. It will help lead to a very successful and rewarding career."

Sharon Bialy, Artios Award Winning Casting Director, Bialy/Thomas Casting, *Barry, The Handmaid's Tale, Breaking Bad, Better Call Saul*

"You want to be an ACTOR. Hold onto your hat and be prepared to sharpen your business skills too. Acting is a business and you are the principal asset. Yes, you need to develop your craft, but that's just the beginning. Networking is essential, but understanding the business of entertainment is even more important. You must know the players that can enhance your knowledge of the business, as well as influence the choices you make. Yes, it takes a village! This book will give you a clear picture of the steps you will need to take to have a vibrant and sustainable acting career."

Tim McNeal, Head of Creative Talent Development and Inclusion, Disney ABC Television Group

Acting is Your Business

Online resources to accompany this book are available at bloomsbury.pub/acting-business. If you experience any problems, please contact Bloomsbury at: onlineresources@bloomsbury.com

INTRODUCTIONS TO THEATRE

SERIES EDITOR:

JIM VOLZ, CALIFORNIA STATE UNIVERSITY, FULLERTON, USA

This series of textbooks provides a practical introduction to core areas of theatre and performance, and has been designed to support semester teaching plans. Each book offers case studies and international examples of practice, and will equip undergraduate students and emerging theatre professionals with the understanding and skills necessary to succeed—whether in study or in the entertainment industry.

Directing Professionally: A Practical Guide to Developing a Successful Career in Today's Theatre
Kent Thompson
ISBN 978-1-4742-8876-7

Get the Job in the Entertainment Industry: A Practical Guide for Designers, Technicians, and Stage Managers
Kristina Tollefson
ISBN 978-1-3501-0378-8

Introduction to the Art of Stage Management: A Practical Guide to Working in the Theatre and Beyond
Michael Vitale
ISBN 978-1-4742-5720-6

Introduction to Arts Management
Jim Volz
ISBN 978-1-4742-3978-3

The Art of Scenic Design: A Practical Guide to the Creative Process
Robert Mark Morgan
ISBN 978-1-3501-3954-1

The Art of Writing for the Theatre: An Introduction to Script Analysis, Criticism, and Playwriting
Luke Yankee
ISBN 978-1-3501-5557-2

Writing for Stage and Screen: Creating a Perception Shift in the Audience
Sherry Kramer
ISBN 978-1-3503-3826-5

Acting is Your Business

How to Take Charge of Your Creative Career

Wendy S. Kurtzman

methuen | drama

LONDON • NEW YORK • OXFORD • NEW DELHI • SYDNEY

METHUEN DRAMA
Bloomsbury Publishing Plc
50 Bedford Square, London, WC1B 3DP, UK
1385 Broadway, New York, NY 10018, USA
29 Earlsfort Terrace, Dublin 2, Ireland

BLOOMSBURY, METHUEN DRAMA and the Methuen Drama logo are trademarks of
Bloomsbury Publishing Plc

First published in Great Britain 2024
Reprinted 2025

A catalogue record for this book is available from the British Library.

Library of Congress Cataloging-in-Publication Data
Names: Kurtzman, Wendy S., author.
Title: Acting is your business : how to take charge of your creative career /
Wendy S. Kurtzman.
Description: London ; New York : Methuen Drama, 2024. |
Series: Introductions to theatre | Includes bibliographical references and index.
Identifiers: LCCN 2023018978 (print) | LCCN 2023018979 (ebook) |
ISBN 9781350385795 (hardback) | ISBN 9781350385788 (paperback) |
ISBN 9781350385801 (pdf) | ISBN 9781350385818 (ebook)
Subjects: LCSH: Acting–Vocational guidance.
Classification: LCC PN2055 .K87 2024 (print) | LCC PN2055 (ebook) |
DDC 792.02/8023—dc23/eng/20230713
LC record available at https://lccn.loc.gov/2023018978
LC ebook record available at https://lccn.loc.gov/2023018979

ISBN: HB: 978-1-3503-8579-5
        PB: 978-1-3503-8578-8
        ePDF: 978-1-3503-8580-1
        eBook: 978-1-3503-8581-8

Series: Introductions to Theatre

Typeset by RefineCatch Limited, Bungay, Suffolk
Printed and bound in Great Britain

To find out more about our authors and books visit www.bloomsbury.com
and sign up for our newsletters.

To my students, the best teachers I know.

Contents

Introduction 1

Part I The Boardroom

1 Meet the Boardroom 15

5 Head of Marketing/Branding 73

6 Head of Business Development (Biz Dev) 95

7 Head of Representation 107

8   Head of Creative Development   123

9   Head of Outreach   133

10   Putting It All Together   143

Part II Industry Insights

11 Casting FAQ

12 Interviews: Let's Get Down to Business

Illustrations

How to use this book

This book will give you a step-by-step action plan to organize your company and clarify your strategies. The book delivers worksheets, templates, and case studies. In every chapter there is a chance to further your learning by completing the worksheets and/or using the icon ⌐ to navigate to the available on-line resources. I have linked this book to some valuable industry guides that are only accessible to those "in the know." These are the guides and resources currently used in our industry, such as guidelines for intimacy coordinators and artists, financial planning information from a former actress turned financial planner who I met while working with the Entertainment Community Fund (formerly known as The Actors Fund), and links to Therapist Aid which provides a myriad of worksheets for mental wellness and new ways to reframe our thinking in challenging situations. I highly encourage unpacking this book, seat by seat, and completing each chapter's imperatives before moving on to the next. There will be a constant retuning and reprioritizing as you learn to articulate your mission and vision for your company.

I have also included graphics to give you a visual representation of your boardroom and the various departments that comprise the "Business of YOU, inc." Having a visual model articulates the harmony between your various tasks and enterprises. It allows you to see that each department has a distinct "seat at the table." One objective is no more important than another. The idea is to learn how to keep all these departments working in tandem. The end of the book gives you a visual calendar/schedule to help you start a time management system. It allows for a schedule that recognizes the ever-changing variables of a creative career and honors the more consistent ones like mental health, the job(s) you have to support yourself, and the opportunity to grow as an individual and citizen, not just as an artist.

In Part II of the book entitled "Industry Insights," I have included Casting FAQs and a chapter called "Interviews: Let's Get Down to Business." There are conversations with casting directors in the United States, Australia, Germany, and the UK, addressing diversity in casting, motion capture casting, and casting specific to their geography. There are coaches and advocates who share their theories and opinions, and there is an interview with an intimacy coordinator that further expands on-set protocol for actors and affirms a personal "Bill of Rights."

Overall, I would encourage you to look carefully at the table of contents and unpack this book chapter by chapter. It is meant to be your working guide and to serve as a constant advocate for your job as an actor/artist.

INVICTUS

By William Ernest Henley

Out of the night that covers me,
Black as the pit from pole to pole,
I thank whatever gods may be
For my unconquerable soul.

In the fell clutch of circumstance
I have not winced nor cried aloud.
Under the bludgeonings of chance
My head is bloody, but unbowed.

Beyond this place of wrath and tears
Looms but the Horror of the shade,
And yet the menace of the years
Finds and shall find me unafraid.

It matters not how strait the gate,
How charged with punishments the scroll,
I am the master of my fate,
I am the captain of my soul.

Introduction

How it all started

As part of my job as a casting director, I regularly attend and watch online college showcases of graduating seniors from BFA and MFA classes. Years back, after a particular showcase for a prestigious university, I heard my colleagues, who are other entertainment industry professionals, make the following comments:

"What was that?"
"The material . . ."
"What were they thinking?"
"They are not leaning into who they are or what makes them unique!"

The comments were discouraging. Worst of all, as a casting professional with over 35 years of experience, I agreed. I attended showcases for many years to expand my casting arsenal and meet emerging talent for films, limited series, and television movies. At the time, I was working steadily for two prominent television producers and was starting to get more opportunities in feature films. I saw the expectations of these young artists and felt the hopeful anxiety behind this moment of truth where if all went well, they could leave with representation and an entrée into the casting world. Truthfully, it doesn't really work that way.

The academic system for BFAs and MFAs is an amazing training ground for craft development and a great place to create community. But when it comes to actually helping the students with concrete ways to navigate the business, there is a disconnect. I have seen first hand as I have worked with many notable universities, that there is little investment in post college career advice. Furthermore, acting for the stage has specific nuances that differ from acting for the camera. Put these two blind spots together and you have actors leaving these programs with little to no content developed, and no idea how to effectively market the materials they do have. The business feels elusive and the artists feel daunted and even unworthy of professional attention.

I started writing this book after my first few years of teaching in academia, where I realized that this demographic of emerging artists—the very worthy and well poised BFA and MFA students entering the marketplace—needed to learn how to navigate the specifics of the industry and manage their expectations in order to achieve success in their chosen field. Whether they were in programs dedicated to acting for stage or film, the blind spots were the same: they weren't learning how to present their skills to the marketplace; how to manage their development, expectations, and opportunities; and how to have a healthy relationship with the career they've selected.

As my work progressed and my understanding of my vision deepened, I came to realize that this book is really for any artist who has chosen a profession that does not have a linear path. That can include dancers, visual artists, directors, writers, and of course actors.

There's no straight path or definite route that will take you to a place of success. It varies for every individual. This book is for the creative, brave, hungry, strong, and fearless individuals— young, old, and anywhere in between—who want to stay true to the burning fire of passion in their bellies.

What this book will help you achieve

You've trained and studied for years. You've earned a degree. Now what? The number one question facing emerging artists is, "How do I get a job and have a career as an actor?" Throughout my years in the industry, I have read many "how-to" books by my colleagues. They all offer useful advice. But the one book I've always thought would be most useful—a kind of paint-by-numbers tool kit—was missing. There was no proactive daily approach for managing the life of an artist, for creating order in a sometimes very chaotic career choice. So here it is!

This book addresses this fundamental yet often neglected aspect of the non-linear creative journey. It delivers a precise formula for emerging artists to organize and manage the next chapter of their lives allowing them to be proactive about building a career. It provides them with the tools they'll need to connect with agents, managers, writers, directors, and casting directors to find work.

If acting is your business, you must run it as a business. This book positions the artist as the CEO of their own company with a boardroom table as a visual model. At that table are seven other key positions, each representing an area of action and expertise, which the CEO must understand and manage to be able to build a successful career. This book is based on the syllabus I've been teaching and is the result of many years of interaction between students, professors, and industry professionals to address the fundamental needs of emerging artists. My students have told me that the action plan in this book works. I know it can help you achieve your goals, too.

If acting is your business, you must understand the business of acting: this is an imperative that most creatives ponder, but don't intrinsically understand. You have to determine your business's goals as well as the job duties required to achieve those goals. You must learn how to wear all the different hats necessary for those duties. Further, the entertainment industry itself is also a network of business professionals. Learning what their jobs are, how they function, and how they interact with each other is crucial.

This book serves as a template for career management. It will give you tentpoles to structure your personal "business" as an actor. It will give you strategies for integrating with managers, agents, casting directors, and producers. It will help you determine your brand. When an actor creates a strong brand and sense of purpose/mission, fellow professionals will partner and collaborate. This book also speaks to the challenges of living a creative life, offers proactive ways to navigate a non-linear career choice, and is a practical guide for how to understand and anticipate what the industry wants from you. It's designed to be used both when you're getting started as well as a refresher whenever certain aspects of your career need recalibration.

I say it is a prescriptive book because if you needed help with a health issue, a doctor would write a prescription. Think of this book in the same way. It will help you set up systems which you will then need to stick to. In order for it to work, you need to fill the prescription and then follow protocol!

Why do emerging artists need systems and structure in their daily lives? A colleague summed it up perfectly in a meeting: "What are you going to do now that it's Tuesday at 11:00am?" In other words, without a destination to a daily job, the idea of empty space and no schedule to adhere to can leave you feeling daunted and untethered. I once heard an interview with a very prolific director who put it simply: "Without structure, you go mad." This book will help with that structure. Your years are no longer defined in the increments that high school and university presented. It's a career now and for most, it doesn't happen in fixed increments. This will have to be a time of readjustment and balance. This book will help you achieve that balance between your creative dreams and the practicalities of day-to-day life. Paying bills and keeping yourself afloat is just as noble a mission as booking a commercial. Developing material that showcases your versatility is just as important as getting an agent or getting a job.

This is are especially true in the beginning of a career. From my experience, students in academia are hungry for more connection to the professional world. They want to learn about the industry, they want to know how to ready themselves for the demands of a large and sometimes undefinable industry. They want to start developing film/video of themselves, they want to learn self-taping skills, they want to make connections and learn the etiquette of business correspondence. They want to be proactive but don't know how. And when you don't know how to do something, that makes you uncomfortable. People tend to lean into what makes them comfortable and neglect the rest. I see this with artists all the time. They'd rather not deal with the hard stuff, whatever is not creative work. But you are a business. There will be non-creative tasks, and if you don't deal with them, who will?

Don't let this freak you out! Not only is it possible for you to handle all of these roles, but your collection of tasks will actually be easier to achieve once you have delineated them and created a game plan. Most importantly, this process will give you a sense of control in a career where most things are out of your control.

I guarantee this book will change your life

Every time I get a call or email from an actor asking for my time and advice, we wind up talking about the same thing: control. We discuss three aspects of it. We list what is out of their control, so they can remember to release anxiety about these things. Then we discuss what is in their control, so they can identify tasks that will further their career that don't require someone else's greenlight. Finally, we talk about how they will take control to actually achieve these tasks. This book does the same thing. As a result, it will reduce your anxiety and help you feel more proactive. After reading this book and instituting new systems and outlooks, you will never again be a leaf in the wind.

Ever seen a leaf in the wind? It blows wherever the breeze takes it. It has no chance to set its own course or question its destination. The industry will present you with opportunities to achieve your goals as well as distractions from your goals. Sometimes it will be hard to tell the difference between the two and that's how we lose our way. When you couple this confusion with fear—fear of rejection, fear of not working, fear of aging out of a job, fear of not getting an agent, etc.—you have a formula for an unfocused career that blows you about wherever the wind takes you and ultimately leads to malaise and discouragement.

There are going to be times when the power to say "no" and stay put will be the right decision. Don't run all over trying to be all things at once. Slow down, be selective, focused, and purposeful. Set your intention. When you're organized and proactive, you will always proceed with purpose. You will never feel lost and overwhelmed. I made a strong choice to enter academia while I was still working in the professional world. I wanted to give the students access to my contacts, knowledge, and demystify this crazy creative journey. I knew that purpose would open new doors not only for the students, but for me. And it has. It's led me to more casting jobs, revitalized my industry contacts, and given me a renewed sense of direction.

There are many ways to get where you're going. Anyone who claims to have all the answers is full of "you know what!" People follow all sorts of methodologies. Some are effective and some aren't. Heck, some artists call upon the universe to tell them how to proceed. That's cool. I'm not one to judge. But there are things the universe can't tell you, such as what to do during the down time, when you're not at an audition or working on a set. And it definitely doesn't tell you how to convince the industry that you are a worthy and talented actor who deserves a shot. So, proceeding with that as a fact, let's try this method of managing your career. Either the Universe will say "hell yeah" or it won't, but you won't know until you try.

Acting is *your* business—casting is *mine*

This book is specifically designed by someone who has an insider's view. My casting career, which has spanned more than 35 years, started in episodic television. I worked for independent offices before being courted by a network to be an executive of dramatic casting. Eventually, I left that job to start my own company, where I was able to focus on what brings me the most joy: discovering and nurturing talent.

Being on the other side of the desk, I gained perspective and insight into not only the audition process but the choices and attitudes that came into the room during those auditions. The hardest part was watching actors balance the need to stay professional with the profound need to book the job. Projecting "need" in the room robs an actor of their power. Some call it "casual indifference," some just frame it as a chance to reconnect with what they love and use the time to explore and play. Interestingly, it's an attitude but it's also a sense of power or purpose that ultimately turns heads.

This book challenges artists to find purpose and strength in all areas of their creative life. It strives to encourage a whole artist and citizen of the world. That is your business as well. Not just learning lines or making strong choices, but being the most expansive and aware artist you can be. That's why it's worth naming it as a business and investing in it. This is why I liken this creative journey to a boardroom and a CEO running those important meetings. I work with actors everyday to help them shape their creative journeys. I show them how to embrace this ideology and use it to stay positive and focused. The results achieved through teaching and coaching proved this system was working long before this book was published!

You are the master of your universe

You can't avoid the "school of hard knocks" but you can learn where your academic education is serving you and where there are places to grow, improve, and learn. Use this book to take charge and make a commitment to manage your career with attention and care.

Remember that your creativity and the way you present it is uniquely yours. No one can take it from you and no one can duplicate it. The flip side of that coin? No one else can create your career for you. Design the atmosphere of a thriving company and be the master of that universe. That may feel overwhelming, but you already have everything you need for the journey. The rest will come. I believe that wholeheartedly and I have seen the results.

Business + artistry = balanced creative career: they are not mutually exclusive. An acting career is equal parts talent and business acumen. To be successful and purpose driven, both objectives must get equal attention. Getting comfortable with this concept is crucial. Create a mindset of a working professional that will still allow connection to your unique brand of artistry. If an actor understands the business and uses the information available to them, it only empowers them as an artist.

Treat your acting career as a startup looking for investors: just as a startup must "boot strap" in the beginning, so must an actor. With a focus on finances, mental and physical health, creative and business development, representation, marketing and branding, and a sense of self beyond an acting career, an actor can create a robust company and be a CEO with vision and purpose!

Before we get started

When I read books on the industry, I need to trust the person guiding me. I want more context about who they are and whether or not they have a relatable journey to mine. So before we dig in, here's my story as well as a testimonial from one of my students.

Who is this Wendy person?

My hyphenate reads Singer–Fashion Stylist and Multiline Clothing Rep– Casting Director–Mother–Founder of College to Career Acting–Professor– Actress. It's been a windy and exciting road!

My journey started in high school, as it does for most aspiring actresses. I wanted to be a musical theatre actress and move to New York City. Then came my first pivot: my parents had no intention of sending their 17-year-old to New York City, so I went to the only other school I had applied to: UCLA.

Upon graduation, I had no idea what to do or how to navigate the industry. There had been no instruction offered or directives given that addressed the transition from academia. My answer was to leave LA. I figured if I had to start somewhere it should be in a place with a lot of musical theatre opportunities. Meanwhile, I took a side job working in fashion. Eventually, I bought a ticket to New York and planned to stay on my friend's couch until I could get the lay of the land.

Enter pivot number two: while still in LA, I was cast in an Equity production of *Fiddler on the Roof*. After ten weeks of playing to dinner-theatre crowds, the producers asked us all to stay on for four more weeks and offered us Equity cards in return. Now I was an Equity actress and auditioning for shows. I still really wanted NYC but realized it was more important to be working, and that meant staying where I was.

Pivot number three: I had my sideline jobs as a salesgirl in a fancy department store by day and as a waitress at night. Then the salesgirl job turned into something more, and I felt like having a second career in fashion was not a bad idea. I leaned into fashion and learned how to run a multiline showroom. I traveled twice a year to San Francisco with the lines and made a name for myself in the "C" building of the California Mart. Pretty soon, I had set my sights on a better job: the West Coast Rep for Jones of New York. It wasn't what I had planned to do, but I loved it—and hey, at least I would finally put New York on my resumé!

Shortly thereafter came pivot number four: I realized I didn't want a career in fashion. I didn't want to travel from state to state with lines of clothing because it was very solitary and I missed my community. I missed the energy of the creative industry and the rush of being with performers. So I took my skills from running a showroom and applied for a Casting Internship at Reuben Cannon casting.

I told a very angry boss at Jones of New York that I would not be taking the job and two weeks later, I was working in a busy multi-show casting office for a prolific producer named Steven J. Cannell. His shows included *The A-Team, Hunter, Hardcastle and Mc Cormick, 21 Jump Street and many others.* I worked for a casting director named Karen Vice and read with actors in auditions whenever the opportunity arose. I also worked on a soap opera called Santa Barbara, where a young actress, Robin Wright, was getting her start.

My training as an actress was paying off. I was a good reader, I understood character development in the scripts and I was insatiable in my quest to learn about (and cast) every great actor out there. My main boss, Reuben Cannon, was a fantastic mentor. After he assigned me to work with Karen as an assistant, he did something that changed my life and the course of my career. He tagged me as his assistant on a Spielberg movie he was going to cast called *The Color Purple.*

Working on that film, I fell madly, deeply in love with the casting process. I won't bore you with all of the details of my professional life. There's IMDb for that! Suffice it to say I've had a fantastic career. I worked with smart, creative producers and directors and I learned things about acting that I would never have known without being on the other side of the desk.

When my third child was born, I had been casting for 20 years. My life was so busy at this point. I was barely managing. Then came pivot number five: I had to take a step back from a career that was everything to me.

It was hard. For the next nine years, I was a full-time wife and mother. I raised my kids, was a full-time driver (pre-Uber!) and a short-order cook. I kept my love of casting alive by continuing to learn new talent and by attending the showcases of the BFA and MFA classes entering the industry.

In 2013, I attended the showcase I refered to earlier. After hearing my colleagues' remarks, I had an epiphany and along came pivot number six: I wanted to start a business to help actors transition from academia to the industry. That is how "College to Career Acting" was born. My goal was to give behind the scenes access to all facets of the industry. To create community, opportunity and connect fellow creatives.

From the development and success of that program, I became fully immersed as a professor. I have taught at many distinguished universities across the country. I quickly learned that academia is not run the way the business world demands. In fact, there were so many times I felt frustrated by the lack of support for the most obvious collaborations and resources.

However, ultimately, I realized that universities are run by provosts and chairpersons who have fiscal concerns that outweigh anything else. Meanwhile, the students still had not been encouraged to develop a sense of autonomy and use resources that were right at their fingertips. My time inside academia was valuable. In fact, that would be a good title for another book: "Inside Academia: The Untold and Uncovered Truths of BFA and MFA Programs." But my goal is not to change the system.

Being on faculty gave me the information and perspective I had been missing. It showed me very clearly where there are holes in the system and what links are missing between education and the industry. It is where I developed the concept and visual model for this book, specifically designed by someone who has an insider's view.

Now ... remember I mentioned "actress" as the final piece of my hyphenate? That's because after this long journey, I finally know what it takes, and understand what I have that is unique to me and my sensibility. I know how to market myself as an actress and walk into a room with confidence. That is because after all these years, I understand this business ... inside and out. I have the skills and tools to create a busy, productive, and successful career. This knowledge has brought me the power to develop myself as an artist in countless ways as well. Meanwhile, I continue to work with actors to help them shape their creative journeys.

Student testimonial

I first met Wendy through zoom in a BFA Acting Industry class at Pace University in New York City. When she began presenting the idea of treating our careers like a boardroom, I remember everything in my body resisted. Wendy pushed us early on to come to the table with our most authentic selves, the things that made each of us unique. She wanted us to get super specific and micro with our industry "types" and taglines. She urged us to either come up with content or dare to begin the process of executing projects we'd always wanted to make but were pushing off until "later." We were basically afforded the chance to work through this book first-hand.

Through all of this, I found myself shutting down and shutting out. Spending two years in a boarding school drama program and then another four in a college conservatory setting bred a kind of mentality I think is often found in academia that hadn't been challenged yet in my life. I was focused on being what I thought was a "very serious actor." I wanted to be as broad as possible in order to play as many parts as possible. In the years prior to meeting Wendy, I played a one-legged man, a Shakespearean fool, several ingenues, and a soccer player. I was happy with that. When Wendy asked what my type was, I didn't want to be specific because I didn't want to limit myself. When we were supposed to come to class with vision statements about where we wanted our careers to go, mine was broad and along the lines of "audition until I get a job." I brought several ideas I had about queer films I wanted to make to class, but I explained I didn't want to make them anytime soon because I didn't want to pigeonhole myself as a queer person in the industry.

It was around this time that Wendy and I had a one-on-one meeting that changed everything for me. Prior to this meeting I was explaining my frustrations about the class to my partner. I told her I was upset that this professor was making me put myself into a box and focus on creating content when I should be auditioning. My partner stopped me and asked why I was being so stubborn. When I couldn't answer right away, I knew the problem was most likely fear. I was scared of being limited. I was scared that those personal things about myself would mean I could only exist as one thing in the industry. I thought that spending time on a creative project I was passionate about would take away from being an actor. I brought those fears to Wendy in our one-on-one meeting, and she looked at me and said, "Emma, I'm here to support you but also challenge you. You need to change your perspective. Those things won't limit you … They're your superpowers and the reason you will succeed. Nothing is mutually exclusive in this business.

Actors pivot and grow from all different experiences, success comes in many forms and the most important piece is to not only stay true to who you are but know that you can be the master of your universe."

What I didn't see then that I do now after more time with Wendy and a month in an LA intensive meeting with many other industry professionals is that this business *is* personal. You have to bring yourself to it. If the industry doesn't know where specifically to put you in the beginning, you'll get thrown into a big general pile and never get out. Every single person I have met in the industry since Wendy's class has said the same things. The more specific you are, the better shot you have. People want to know your essence. The most exciting thing right now is authenticity and truth. Also, Wendy was absolutely right. Everyone wants to know what you're creating and working on outside of an audition. It's clear to me now that not only does this *not* take away from acting, but it shows you're a person with goals and passions outside of the audition room.

Throughout the LA intensive, Wendy and I kept sharing knowing glances when someone would say something that directly related to this book, and the things Wendy shared with us in class. What I came away with is that treating your acting career like a business and being as specific and intentional as possible with each part of that business is universally acknowledged in the industry as the most successful path forward. Not only did it feel great to have this knowledge reaffirmed by so many other voices, but it lit a fire in my soul to know that all of these tools are ones I now own for myself. I don't have to keep checking in with someone or constantly asking for favors that aren't mutually beneficial. I can fully design and forge a career for myself by myself—with the help of a network and support system, of course—that works towards exactly what I want to do and who I want to be in this industry.

That feeling is golden as a young artist stepping into this business.

Emma Jean. Pace University, BFA Class of 2022

Now let's get to work

I've told you about me, now let's dig into you. It's time to embark on this journey and get your startup on its feet. Let's meet the members of your boardroom.

Part I

The Boardroom

1

Meet the Boardroom

The following is a graphic of your boardroom table. Each seat represents facets/departments of your creative career. The CEO is sitting at the top seat.

This book is about creating what I call the artist's boardroom. Every artist has their own C-suite of sorts behind their successful creative career. There's the CEO, CFO, Head of HR, Head of Marketing & Branding, Head of Creative Development, Head of Business Development, Head of Representation, and Head of Community Work & Outreach. The only difference for emerging artists, is that all these key players are YOU.

Seat 1: The CEO

The CEO is the most senior corporate position. The person with the power to make important creative, financial, and executive decisions. The force behind a successful company. The brains and the brawn. Well, guess what? That is YOU! You are the CEO of your company. Every day you get to make decisions that will strategically move your business forward and further realize your vision.

However, CEO's don't do it alone! With capital and investors behind them, they hire capable and talented people to help them organize and execute their mission. This is their Board of Directors, which in this book we will call "The Boardroom".

When you are an actor or creative artist, unless you have access to unlimited funds or have already achieved commercial success, you do not have a team of employees working on your behalf. So, who needs to do these important jobs that create and support your career? YOU! Until there is enough money to hire these individuals or enough work to pay the percentages, all the jobs at this highly successful company are your responsibility.

The coolest thing about being CEO of your career is that it puts you in control. Much of an actor's life feels dependent. It seems like others—who do or don't call you in for auditions, cast you, sign you as a client, write about you in the press, give you extra lines, or edit the final cut—have all the power. I am here to tell you that nothing is further from the truth. YOU have power. YOU are the badass in charge of an exciting, growing, unicorn of a start-up company and this book will help you take it public.

As we will discuss in depth in the next chapter, your two biggest jobs as CEO are to create vision and mission statements, and to move your company toward your goals by making sure the needs of every other department are met. With that, let's meet the other seats at the boardroom table.

Seat 2: The CFO

The head of finances, or Chief Financial Officer, is the most important and also the most dreaded position to fill. I can tell you now, from the vast experience I have had, that this area causes the most stress and discomfort for actors/artists. But it doesn't have to! Money is not a dirty word. It is a necessity and a means to an end. Your relationship with it will determine your ability to sustain and survive the life of an actor/artist.

Not only will I help you grasp and achieve your essential duties as CFO but I'll also teach you how to change your entire mindset around money so you can achieve a sense of well-being and freedom. When you take on an active role as the CFO of your company, you will be working from a place of strategy and accountability that will empower you to charge ahead in your performing career without fear.

The CFO's main job is to manage the money. This starts by creating a budget and managing it over time. The job also involves sourcing income strategically, paying bills, and setting and attaining goals for creative expenses. A successful CFO minimizes stress . . . making the next executive's job much easier.

Seat 3: Head of Human Resources

Human Resources, or HR, performs human resource management. In a large company it oversees hiring, wage disputes, and performance evaluation. It also is a department that deals with discrimination, employee motivation, and can serve as a place of mediation for internal disputes.

Why do you need an HR department? Because YOU are responsible for the health and welfare of your most valued employee . . . YOU! The head of HR's number one goal is to maintain a productive employee.

As an actor, your mind and body are your most valuable resources. There are few other lines of work in which productivity is more directly linked to physical and mental health. If you don't feel great—ambitious, motivated, and ready—you won't book the job. And if you don't look your best . . . well, we are in a visual business. Type, style, flair, and the external appearance you create is a lasting first impression.

But the Head of HR is responsible for even more, connecting you to mentors for advice, navigating work permits and visa issues and supporting you during times of potential discrimination. Think of this board room seat as a real-talk fairy godmother: The Head of HR is a watchdog for your well being, always has your best interests at heart, and supports your instincts.

Seat 4: Head of Marketing & Branding

How many times have you heard these words applied to the acting profession? You're an artist and may feel that the concepts of marketing are "reductive" at best, and at worst, the concept of branding as "practices only to be used for cattle." Fortunately, your Head of Marketing & Branding knows that's not true. Marketing and branding are not bad words, just overused and generally misunderstood.

Strategically used, this seat at the table is not only crucial but can give aspiring artists a lot of satisfaction, control, and pride. It can be a tool used to creatively express facets of their personalities and social lives, and show their aesthetic takes on their surroundings.

This exec understands that exposure is the key to success. How can casting directors call you in for auditions if they don't know you exist or how to find you? Not only do industry professionals expect you to market yourself, they'll admire it when you do so successfully, because that suggests dedication, innovation, and self-awareness, all of which are desirable qualities in an actor.

To this end, your Head of Marketing & Branding will be your biggest supporter. This executive will help you pivot your approach, so that you see your digital presence as an artistic playground rather than a mercenary obligation. First, this Head will respond to the industry's demand that you determine your brand. Next is the task of building content—e.g. a website,

Instagram posts, reels—to support that brand. Finally, this Head will have a strategy to market you and your content, and give industry professionals the opportunity to respond and react to that content. Along the way, you will develop your unique perspective and come to understand why you stand out, all of which leads to booking the job!

Seat 5: Head of Business Development (Biz Dev)

A long, long time ago, there was a circular file that sat on a desk, filled with cards called a Rolodex. People couldn't live without one. It organized contacts and grew with you as you found more success and more connections within your business. The reason it was useful is because it was organized and the entries were descriptive.

Today, we all have thousands of contacts in our phones. But which ones are important as we carve out the career we want? Your Head of Biz Dev will create and maintain your database of contacts and also manage correspondence with them, including knowing when to publicize which projects and to whom. Further, this board member is responsible for generally keeping you connected and informed.

Basically, the Head of Biz Dev is a great conversationalist because they're always up on current events, never forgets a name, and knows how to make everyone feel like the most important person in the room.

Seat 6: Head of Representation

Every actor I speak to asks, "Can you help me get a manager or agent?" And I reply, "Let me ask a question: What have you done that makes you ready for representation?"

A false belief persists that with representation, doors will open and access will be granted to all sorts of elusive opportunities. In fact, more often than not, artists sign with managers and agents after they've developed materials and have already started booking jobs. It is incumbent upon all actors to work and advocate on their own behalf.

Agents and managers are only a valuable component once you have content and a body of work for them to "sell." An agent or manager is a partner: They don't work for you, but with you. This means that even after you have them, guess who's still running the show? That's right: YOU. So you may as well start now.

This section will teach you where to look for places to submit yourself, how to read breakdowns and know if they're right for you, how to self-tape or self-submit, and how to handle any meetings you might get as a result.

Seat 7: Head of Creative Development

Worried about access to opportunity? Create your own opportunities. Every production company employs creative development executives. They find and identify stories and ideas worthy of turning into scripts. The business has shifted to a new paradigm where anyone can create, produce, shoot, and release a project for public consumption, so there is nothing stopping YOU from making a short film or web series. This is great because with you as the casting director, you are guaranteed to get a role (if you want one)!

Your Head of Creative Development will find and develop stories that showcase your talents—along the way, you'll also pick up valuable skills as a writer, director, producer, or all of the above, which will enhance your knowledge of the industry. Your stories are waiting to be told!!

Seat 8: Head of Outreach

What?? Why is there an Outreach seat at this table—what does that have to do with an acting career?

Most aspiring actors have very strong agendas: "I need to get cast in a project," "get that audition," "get an agent," and on and on. All of that is a one-way street. It is about what you need and want. This is the one seat that is not about YOU. Instead, it needs your passion and energy towards what others need.

Your Head of Outreach understands the importance of real communication and of giving without an agenda. But, fine, ok: You "need" to know how this will serve you. This business is collaborative. When you ask yourself what others need, how you can fit into their framework, and what you can offer, it creates new opportunities and opens doors to creative, intelligent, and passionate people—but that only happens when you truly, honestly have no agenda.

Be a connector!! Get to a place where you truly are not thinking about whether or not it comes back around. Put your needs aside and GIVE WITH NO AGENDA.

That's your boardroom!

The boardroom is a "YES." It is your opportunity to check-in with yourself in order to strategize and grow. It's a dinner party with all your favorite people—smart, creative, resourceful people—and it all lives in YOU! Each seat holds a facet of your personality and character. The next step will be examining each seat at the table in closer detail.

2

The CEO

The CEO's role is to keep the company always moving closer to its main objective. As the CEO of your company, this means you have three basic job duties.

- **Act as a figurehead.** Every time you leave the house, you represent your brand. You must be able to articulate your vision and mission. Further, you're the one who's accountable for success or failure.
- **Determine your incremental goals.** Clearly define the steps that will lead you toward achieving your vision. Then keep them in mind when making every single decision.
- **Ensure department needs are met.** CEOs spend all day in meetings—with the other people in seats at the boardroom table—to help prioritize immediate and long- term goals.

Let's dig in.

Act as a figurehead

The CEO is the name and face of the company. The persona that's created around that title tells the world who you are and what your company stands for. You have chosen a public career. Representing you and your "company" are synonymous. If you want to give priority and structure to what you want to accomplish, naming it, giving it either a real or fictitious LLC status will encourage you to think differently about acting as a profession. It makes it professional. It makes it a company you are running and are proud of.

CEO—Image

Therefore, it's important to create a CEO Image that is singular to you and your style. The way you present yourself, the interests you have, and your artistic sensibility are all tied together and part of the image you are projecting to your audience.

It is crucial to dial into a very real and authentic representation of how you walk through this world. This means giving serious thought to the details of your personal image, paying attention to your quirks, habits, varied interests, world views, passions, etc … They are reflected in the way we style ourselves and the way we interact with others and instill interest and confidence. Some people are very adept at this concept and others struggle to define themselves. When it works, there is no stopping what can be achieved.

We have all been in meetings before when someone walks into the room and we make an assessment or evaluation of that person based on our perception of image, persona, or style. What kind of energy comes at us? What is in their image that gives us visual information? Tailored, bohemian, rocker grunge, and kitschy all tell us something. Trustworthy, competent, interesting. We make these decisions in a split second and those decisions either inspire us or warn us. If they are not clear and we can't figure it out, we tune out and don't invest or lean in. We want and tend to trust our visual assessment and first impression.

If you present strongly and honor who you really are through your sense of style and self, it will inspire others and project confidence. Whether you are a jeans and baseball cap kinda person or someone who is up on trends and fashion, there is an opportunity to create a strong sense of recognizability. Think of artists in the music business and how they give us a view of their unique selves. Their senses of style are an iconic part of their personas: Billie Eilish, Lizzo, Elton John, Beyonce, H.E.R., Harry Styles, Lady Gaga … you get the point.

After all, part of being a FIGUREHEAD means looking and playing the part and if an actor doesn't understand that analogy, who does?

CEO—Vision and mission

Knowing your CEO Image is only part of being a figurehead. Imagine if the CEO of a startup company sat down to pitch an investor and said, "My company doesn't want to pigeonhole itself yet—we can provide any kind of service or product you need!" That would be crazy, right? Yet artists do this kind of thing all the time: they fail to specifically express what they want to do. Mind you, you're just trying to articulate where you want to start. You can change your path at any time. But you have to start somewhere or else the industry won't know what to do with you.

Most artists are multi-talented and layered. In fact, different seats at your board table will be pursuing different aspects of your talents at different times. But the CEO's job is to turn those many layers and talents into one cohesive vision. The CEO does not get distracted by possibilities. The CEO asks and answers two questions: What do you most want and how are you going to get it?

The first question relates to your vision—think of it as your company's vision statement. The second question relates to your game plan—think of it as your company's mission statement. The CEO job requires the creation, strong belief in, and unerring commitment to the goals of your company and the game plan you'll use to get there. As artists, we are always tempted by opportunity the moment it comes our way. The trick is to stay committed to the vision we established and only take advantage of opportunities that fit into our plan.

How do you determine your vision? For most artists, when pressed to articulate a statement, the answers are vague and nonspecific. They will state the objective is to simply be working within their industry, to have a long career in which they are supported by their craft. But when you are emerging, where do you start? There are so many possibilities, but which are realistic at this phase of your career? Where do you initially put your focus and energy in order to reach the point where you are making a living as an actor, musician, or artist?

The vision statement helps clarify this. It is your dream destination. Whether that's doing Shakespeare in regional theatre, becoming a member of a repertory company, working in TV as a sketch actor, carving out a niche in the sci-fi or fantasy world, becoming a voice-over artist, or developing a career as a creator. The vision is the bedrock of your company and all decisions are weighed based on whether or not they support your vision.

Then there's the mission. Every company with a good idea or dream needs to imagine how these goals will be met. It's the creative *how*—how you're going to get there (and the attitude you'll have while you are getting there!). This "how" requires defining incremental goals. If you wanted to make a living as a musician, would you start out by touring with the band, trying to record an album with a band, or building up your credits as a session player? The idea is to pick incremental and specific goals that will lead to success.

Your mission might also affect where you choose to live (if you want to work in regional theatre, it doesn't really matter where you live because you'll take a job wherever the regional theatre hires you). Your finances might dictate where you live, and therefore affect your vision (most aspiring film and TV actors want to be in Los Angeles, but the cash-strapped might prefer an emerging production market such as Atlanta or Albuquerque, which offer lower costs of living).

The path to your objective is determined by whatever puts a fire in your belly. The power behind your passion is what will drive you forward and define you. Since nothing is a guarantee in any artistic industry, why try to emerge on a path you don't want just because you think it's easier? All that does is breed discontent and lower self-esteem. There is virtue in pursuing what you want and supporting the goal in any way that works. Remember the joy. Let that be your guiding force. It's what you can't imagine living without.

Along with identifying joy and passion, you have to focus passion toward one objective and then drive the company toward it. Specificity is the key. A lot of artists say they want to do everything. But if you're pursuing goals on many different paths, then those goals are ultimately competing with each other. You only have so much energy and time (and money!), and now you have split that energy and time between two (or more) paths, instead of going farther along down one path.

Often, actors tell me they are afraid to focus on only one vision and mission, because they think they won't have an opportunity to explore other options down the road. Not only is that not true, but if you don't initially define some kind of vision and mission, you are unlikely to ever get far enough down the road to even have a chance to pivot. No one gets more attention or response than the artist who can succinctly articulate a career vision and mission. This doesn't mean you can never question them. You will have doubts and fears. And sometimes you should act on them! But the time to question everything is not when you've scored a meeting with a producer or have an opportunity to pitch yourself or an idea to a fellow creative.

The reason is twofold: first, no one will think you're capable and confident if you don't think that of yourself. More importantly, industry contacts can't give you help or advice if you don't offer them a plan they can latch onto, add onto, or fit into. As artists, we often feel beholden to all of the gatekeepers who move us forward or backward with a thumbs up or thumbs down. I don't want actors and performers to feel that way. You are just as viable, creative, and strong as any other person in the industry. You have ideas. Take chances on them. The people who succeed are the ones who act on their impulses.

Embrace the great satisfaction that comes from acting on hunches, instinct, and talent. Is it a risk worth exploring and fighting for? Then do it! As CEO, you're the boss and you can make any decision that drives your creative company forward. You don't have to wait for anyone's nod of approval. As the boss, know that the buck stops with you. Yes, in an artistic career, there is a lot outside of your control. But one thing you can control is the expression of and commitment to your artistic vision and mission, and your image. If you are unwilling or unable to do that, your lack of momentum will be no one's fault but your own.

Determine your incremental goals

Even though you'll ultimately be driven by a trust in your creative impulses, you will still need to create schedules and make priorities. Once there is a clear vision for the company, launch a mission that will get you there. All directives can revolve around that and your company can look for and generate projects that support that vision, one at a time. Defining incremental goals in this way will also create purpose.

It's OK for your goals to change—the most successful companies, of course, are the ones that can adapt. Still, you must have one overarching objective at all times. This is your Northstar. Move toward that objective with incremental goals.

I want to break down career goals into two arenas: primary goals and career-adjacent goals (your hyphenate/s). Primary goals inform your hyphenates, which are an extension of your creativity and training, and in turn your hyphenates add nuance to your primary goals.

Primary goals

Let's assume that most of you who are reading this book have chosen a career as an actor. In today's landscape there are many outlets that provide opportunities to act. So, for our purpose we will define *primary* goals as the goals that are directly tied to your career as an actor for hire.

If the primary goal is tied to your vision statement, it may look like this:

1 I am moving to Los Angeles post-graduation and will be seeking non-union commercial work and set experience.
2 I would like to work as an editor as I continue my journey as an actor.
3 I would like to make a name for myself in sketch comedy.
4 I want to be a standup.
5 I want to experience behind the scenes in a casting office or writers room.

6 I want to get a role in a multi-generational series set in middle-America (or Middle Earth!).
7 I want to create dramatic and horror-adjacent TV projects.
8 I want to create children's voice-acting content.
9 I want to collaborate with other BIPOC artists workshopping new musical theatre.

Stylistically speaking, these incremental goals can be tied to the shows you most identify with, the platforms you follow, the genres you relate to, and the types of characters you would be right for. Defining those mission goals will lead you to your objective.

And, of course, your incremental goals include the procuring of and prepping for auditions, the self-submissions, the making of professional contacts, the on-going classes and study . . . in other words, everything that falls into a typical day of an actor's life.

Your job as CEO is to set the goals appropriate to your vision—and then work together with all of the other seats at your boardroom table to achieve those goals. It is not enough to say, "I want to act." That does not benefit you or the other professionals who want to help you with your career.

I believe as do some of my respected colleagues that it's important to "choose a lane" when you first start out. People toss around that phrase a lot. What does it mean?

1. Consider your current look, age, vibe, and skill sets.
2. Then determine how you can use those to fulfill your vision and reach your objective.

It's the same thing I have already been discussing, except now you're also adding in some practicality.

You may be saying, "She's repeating herself," or "This sounds like common sense." Both of those are true. Being a leaf in the wind is the number one mistake made by almost every emerging artist—but not you, if I have any say in it.

Opportunity versus intention, a case study

In New York, I worked with an actress named Isabella, who was comfortable and happy and getting a little bit of work. But after much thought and a lot of strategizing, she decided to move to Los Angeles and start working with an agent, toward the goal of booking TV and film work. Within the first few months of living in LA, an opportunity arose that would take her back to New York. It was for a play. There was no compensation, but the director was asking for her specifically.

She called to seek my advice. During the call, she admitted that the material was not really that compelling to her, but she was very taken with the fact that someone had asked for her to play the lead role without her auditioning. She struggled with the decision of whether or not to move back to New York for the run of the play. I encouraged her to speak to her representation in LA and to remember the reasons she had made the move to LA. I asked her if this opportunity in New York was in line with the goals she had set for herself on the path of her vision. She had to admit that the answer was no. She passed on the play.

In the following weeks, she went out on a number of auditions that introduced her to new casting directors and further fulfilled her ideas of how she would reach the objective to work in film and TV. Some of you might be reading this and thinking, she should've taken the play in New York! Work begets work, and in LA she didn't yet have any work. But if she's auditioning nonstop in LA, that is also work. If you are auditioning, that means offices are interested in you and calling you in.

That is affirmation that you're on the right path. That being said, if she had found the New York play really compelling, maybe the metrics in her decision-making process would have been different. You will face these tough decisions.

Whatever your decision-making process, though, I want you to give extra weight to your calculated bold moves. It was a big deal for Isabella to leave New York and move to LA. I wanted her to honor that risk. And she got representation that wanted to work with her and put her out into the world! That's further affirmation that her risky move was right.

She determined that she wanted to work in LA, she took a bold step toward that vision, and it was already starting to pay off. I did not think she should abandon that win, but rather lean into it and let it play out. About nine months later, she booked a recurring guest starring role in a Netflix series.

Worksheets to Develop and Define Your Goals

Use the following two worksheets as an ongoing method of assessing where you are and holding yourself accountable.

WORKSHEET 1: Creative Goals via the G.S.T. Method

Setting goals can be a daunting task. It feels proactive and initially sustainable and then somehow the motivation starts to slip and slowly the dedication and consistency begin to wane. Before you know it, there has been little forward movement. Therefore, let's create an action plan.

Goals / Steps / Tactics Method

The first tool helps you break it down into three steps:

1 Identify your "Strategic goals".
2 Identify your "Action steps".
3 Identify your "Building tactics".

The "Strategic goal" is your ultimate purpose and destination.

Examples:

- I want to work in film and TV in Los Angeles.
- I want to work in regional theatre.
- I want to start a theatre company.
- I want more on-set experience.

The "Action step(s)" are what you have to do to achieve that goal. What are the key opportunities you need to take advantage of to move this goal forward?

Examples:

- I need to expand my network of business and creative contacts.
- I need to create an accountability group.
- I need to develop my brand.
- I need to create a website.
- I need to create content.
- I need to pick up work as an extra so I can learn what it's like to be on a set.

The "Building tactics" are the pieces that are needed to give you the foundation to execute the goal. These are the working steps to support the actions you will take. What skills, knowledge and capabilities do you need to build that will give you the experience you need? When you know what actions you want to take (e.g., create a website) you can identify the skills you'll need to execute those actions (e.g., website development).

Examples:

- In order to create more content I need to take a class that strengthens my on-camera skills.
- In order to create and work on self-tapes, I need a workable home studio.
- In order to expand my business contacts and generate meetings I need to learn the landscape of the genres I am interested in and identify characters and types I relate to.

WORKSHEET 2: Creative Goals via the S.M.A.R.T. Goals® Method

S.M.A.R.T. Goals® is a registered trademark of Leadership Management® International, Inc.

To get even more specific when determining creative goals, I find the S.M.A.R.T. Goals® Method to be effective. Let's look at that now.

The S.M.A.R.T. Goals® Method
Another tool to help determine long term and incremental goals is the S.M.A.R.T. acronym. I was first made aware of the concept through Peter Drucker's "Management by Objectives." It has been re-purposed and helpful in a variety of fields. I believe it is especially useful to emerging artists. Here is what S.M.A.R.T. stands for:

Specific
Measureable
Achievable
Relevant
Time bound

Let's look at how to craft a S.M.A.R.T. goal by applying each element of S.M.A.R.T. to the following statement:

> "I want to build my career with fellow creatives in the writing and producing arenas."

Specific
Your goal should be clear and specific. Otherwise you will not be able to focus your efforts or feel motivated to achieve it. Try to answer the five "Ws":

Who: Who is involved?

What: What do I want to: accomplish?

When: When do I begin to work on it?

Where: Where is it located? Does it have a specific geographic constraint?

Why: Why is this goal important?

Example: As soon as I graduate, I want to build my career with fellow creatives in the writing and producing arenas. Specifically, I want to work with writers and producers in comedy and those who have worked on shows that deal with LGBTQ issues because those issues are important to me. I want to work with Joey Soloway, wherever there is active production taking place.

Measurable

Measurable goals keep you focused and allow you to track your forward movement. It's a great way to see progress and confirm you are moving in the direction you've chosen.

Example: I want to have at least six new people in my network.

Achievable:

Your goal needs to be realistic and attainable to be successful. It can stretch your abilities but it still needs to remain possible and achievable. Coming through previously overlooked resources or opportunities can bring you closer to this goal.

Questions you might ask: How can I accomplish this goal? How realistic is the goal based on other constraints, i.e. financial factors?

Example: Can I really get six people? Maybe these six are too lofty? Maybe access to that person is not attainable but if I recalibrate and find out who assisted, who worked as a P.A., who has since taken over on the writing team, who is newly hired on the team, I could probably connect with them. These can be contacts that are currently growing in the business with me.

Your recalibrated achievable goal might change to be: I want to build my career with fellow creatives in the writing and producing arenas. Specifically, writers and producers in comedy and those who have worked on shows with LGBTQ issues. I want to work with Joey Soloway. And it is not realistic at this time to work directly with Joey so the achievable goal is six people in the network, including one who can connect me to Joey.

Relevant:
This step is about ensuring your goal matters to you and is in alliance with your other goals.

Example: Specifically, how are these six new contacts relevant to the career you are aiming to create? Maybe three of those writing and producing contacts are more relevant to your current plans and more accessible to learn from. Who will show up for you? Who can be a consistent source of connection and collaboration?

Again, keep refining your goal: I want to build my career with fellow creatives in the writing and producing arenas. Specifically, writers and producers in comedy and those who have worked on shows that deal with LGBTQ issues. I want to add six people to my network, including one who can connect me to Joey Soloway, and I want the remaining contacts to represent writing, acting and producing.

Time bound:
Every goal needs a deadline to focus on and something to work toward. This part of the S.M.A.R.T. criteria prevents your everyday tasks from compromising your long-term goals.

Example: When can this be done? Is it realistic to start when there are other imposing deadlines? Can I afford to give research time to this? If yes, when and how much time?

Now you can articulate your final goal: I want to build my career with fellow creatives in the writing and producing arenas. Specifically, writers and producers in comedy and those who have worked on shows that deal with LGBTQ issues. I want to add six people to my network, including one who can connect me to Joey Soloway, and I want the remaining contacts to represent writing, acting, and producing. I will have this accomplished in one year, or by _____.

Career-adjacent goals: Your hyphenate/s

When I use the word hyphenate, I'm referring to the other occupations and skills you have or embody. Every creative artist is multi-faceted. Your hyphenates are all the pieces of you that are not directly related to your acting per se, but are instead the pieces that make you a more fully realized human being and/or highlight auxiliary talents.

What are your other skills and passions? If you're an actor, are you also a musician, composer, poet, photographer, editor, director, writer, makeup artist, documentarian, dancer, choreographer, life skills coach, special ed teacher, political activist, martial artist, and/or environmentalist? Any of these will add value to your career as a performer. You want to set and achieve goals around these pieces of you as well. Interestingly enough, doing so will make you even more compelling as an actor.

These goals nurture the other parts of you and your talents that bring meaning and satisfaction to your life. These kinds of goals also inform the "Special Skill" section of your resumé, they are other pieces of yourself that can work alongside your acting goals in the industry that ultimately could circle back and lead to acting work. If you're a great editor, your friends may ask you to help with a project and now you're on the production team and you've added five new professionals to your database with whom you have strong relationships. You also have a new perspective on the industry. When you get inside the machine, and see how it works, you can approach it more effectively as an actor.

These non-acting goals can make you an asset to other people, which will help you further expand your skills, connections, and relationships that will ultimately serve you as a performer. Further, of course, when you're making money in a flexible way and on your own terms, you won't have to take a 9–5 job that will keep you from auditioning. While you're waiting to make money at your craft, which may take years, you'll still be in control and creatively fulfilled.

Most important, these are the pieces the industry really looks to grab onto when it's trying to understand your range of talents rather than just the presentational pieces of you. The non-acting sides of you create texture and vitality in your life. It's important to develop your hyphenates based not just on your skills but also your passion: people, including industry professionals, remember you by what you do that you're passionate about, how you move through the world, and how that reflects what you care about in the world at large. Those facets of your hyphenate will also ultimately complement you as an actor.

Once you have set your goals, career and otherwise, you will have to prioritize some over others. That doesn't mean you need to lose some altogether. All your goals are worth noting and assigning to the working departments of your company. Any non-immediate or unarticulated goals can live on the back burner while you lean into the most important goals.

Identify which are immediately accessible and easiest to obtain. Focus the talents you already possess toward each next step. I've had many students tell me that after graduating they are going to write a pilot, create a web series, write a movie script, research for a documentary, create a pod-cast series, etc.

Yet, when pushed to further elaborate, they discover the many aspects that haven't been thought through and the multiple obstacles that will become real problems if they are not identified and tackled. For instance, the idea may be good, but if it requires travel for research, money for collaboration, or the participation of certain friends, then those ideas are only actionable if those details are wrestled to the ground beforehand.

The GOAL in this case is to identify what is immediately actionable and solely within your control. By following the goal you have set, from visualization to articulation to execution, you can definitively clarify whether or not you really have the passion and the bandwidth to make it happen.

WORKSHEET 3: Determining career adjacent goals

This worksheet is meant to help expand what auxiliary talents and training you have as it lends to other creative professions. For example:

If you are a good photographer, maybe it is a skill that can be monetized to take headshots for fellow actors.

If you are a good editor, maybe it can be a useful skill to help fellow actors edit their acting reels.

If you speak a foreign language, maybe there is room to give lessons for anyone trying to learn the language (industry related or not).

Write down all of the auxiliary talents and training you have. Determine which of those bring you the most joy, are the most lucrative, and have the biggest potential market, then take this smaller list, and turn each skill into a career goal.

Now run each goal through either the G.S.T or SMART Method above to determine which is most achievable and makes the most sense for your current needs.

Ensure department needs are met

In order to keep your company always moving toward your Northstar objective, you must constantly check in with the head of every other department, to make sure they are given the time and resources to meet their own goals.

For example, if part of your hyphenate is writing, then that part of your company falls under the purview of your Head of Creative Development. As the CEO, you'll need to meet with your Head of Creative Development to carve out time for those writer goals to be met. It is the CEO's job to manage these inter-department conversations, and validate that part of your artistry. CEOs run the company. They make sure all seats are being heard and that the needs of all seats are being met. If you are the CEO, you spend most of your days in meetings, with the different divisions in your company. Every day you need to check in with these departments. The CEO sets the priorities, so as an artist, you must call consistent company meetings and set your priorities.

Those priorities can shift depending on opportunity and work load. For example if Creative Development is the first priority, then time must be carved out to support the opportunities that department uncovers. But if the workload is overwhelming one week and lightens the following, then the CEO makes the decision to let the other departments meet less often during the first week and then gives extra time to other departments during the second week. Make sense?

Here's the hardest part of the CEO's job: BEING SELECTIVE, HONEST and REALISTIC. You'll also have to exercise time-management skills, because you can't let any one seat monopolize all your time.

In the "Putting It All Together" chapter, we'll explore different scenarios and case studies so you can understand exactly what the push and pull between departments will look like, and how the CEO will make sure all department needs are being met. But I want you to be thinking about this role of the CEO as you read the rest of this book.

If the CEO doesn't hold the team responsible, then no one will. If you choose to lean into an objective and it's not panning out, that has to lead to proactive decisions in other areas of the company.

You are responsible for the momentum and communication between departments.

Closing thoughts

With control comes responsibility. The buck stops with you. No one can make your career successful but you. Work with what you've got. You can't control that you have a different look than the casting director wants or the vision for the project that "went a different way." But you can revel in the fact that you are unique and have a distinct voice. When you embrace the strengths that exist in you and your talent, not only will you always be heading in the right direction, but you will feel less like your career is elusive and controlled by others. It's yours! Honor that, lean into that.

Now that you know who you are and what you want, you'll need a right-hand person to help you keep you in business. Let's meet your CFO.

3

The CFO

Finances are not fun. Unless you are an accounting major or get a thrill from seeing how many ways there are to stretch a limited income, then money probably freaks you out. You're an artist! At the same time, that also means finances may be harder for you than most people, thanks to the freelance and gig nature of your work life — especially considering it could be years before you bring in real income from your art itself.

Credit cards are not the answer. More on that to come — more on that several times throughout, actually, because I cannot say it enough. Credit cards don't buy you time. Rather, they steal time from you.

Fortunately, you're going to learn to be a machine of a CFO. This job is purely analytical. There is no emotion involved in the financial decisions of a successful business. There is either money for a project or there isn't. A project is either over budget, under budget, or right on schedule.

Accountability is key. Ask a Line Producer what happens when there are miscalculations and unforeseen circumstances on a production. Someone's head is on the chopping block! The CFO is the keeper of that accountability. After all they have to answer to the CEO and keep their job! It's no different in the life of an actor.

The main duties of the CFO:

- **Run the books.** Implement a bill-pay system, keep track of your tax-deductible expenses, and keep an emergency fund.
- **Create a timeline for your goals.** Prioritize projects and opportunities, using clear, analytical eyes.
- **Choose sideline jobs strategically.** Why not capitalize on skills you already possess?

The reckoning

Before we dig into the basic job duties of the CFO, let's investigate why this job in particular can be so challenging for actors. Creative artists often struggle to control their finances. I see it all the time — and then their careers suffer as a result. Poor finances lead other areas of their lives to malfunction. Further, they often become too embarrassed and ashamed to reveal the realities of their financial landscape, and before they know it they are trapped in a loop that drives them deeper and deeper into debt.

Denial equals demise. When you are in denial about what you can afford — without incurring debt — you are contributing to the demise of your dream and carefully crafted career.

The majority of the emerging artists I work with fall into three categories: either they are fully supporting themselves, supplementing their income with student loans/scholarships, or supplementing their income with some kind of financial support (from parents, a relative, or a savings account).

Whatever category you fit into, you need to be honest with yourself about how much money is coming in. The industry is expensive and the stakes are high. Expenses associated with classes, headshots, transportation, and time off work to audition will all influence your lifestyle, creative choices and the sacrifices you are willing to make. Be ready to look at the realities of this career — and realize how amazingly entrepreneurial you really are! Lecture over (for now). Let's dig into the three main duties of the CFO.

Run the books

There's not much "how to" in this section. In other words, there is little mystery regarding how to manage your books. It only requires time and attention. I have included this section mostly so I can tell you how important it is that you actually do it. Before you can put money toward your career goals, you must know how much is coming in and going out (and when). Systems are a CFO's best friend.

First, you'll need to implement a bill-pay system. This is the absolute easiest start. There are so many services available online, in addition to apps and even old-school software (e.g. Mint, Quickbooks). Or you can probably use your bank's bill-pay system. The point is to create an accurate account of where your money is spent consistently (e.g. rent, food, transportation, WiFi, union dues, website maintenance, online platforms) and where it is spent for specific opportunities or investments (classes, audition coaching, clothing, headshots). You'll also become aware of cash flow and what times of the month there are more resources available. Actors can and will have income that fluctuates. To achieve financial wellness there must be a cost of living baseline. If a creative artist lives with that baseline as a guide, even when times are flush, there will be less hardship and debt.

Second, do not wait until April to figure out your tax exemptions. Educate yourself on exactly which everyday expenses — auditions, transportation, meals, subscriptions — are tax deductible for you. Then keep track of every single expenditure and how or why it's deductible (you should be able to do much of this in whichever bill-pay system you choose). If you are filing taxes as an independent contractor, it would be advisable to find a tax expert who can help you file quarterly taxes so you are not blindsided with a huge bill when its tax season and filing deadlines are looming. At some point, you may want to speak with a tax specialist about becoming a corporation (an LLC, or S Corp., etc.). There are tax benefits and detriments to incorporating, so the decision will depend on the specifics of your work and expenses.

Third, maintain an emergency fund. Build it slowly and then leave it there. I can't stress this enough. Always have extra cash on hand. Because shit happens. Maybe your roommate kicks you out because his girlfriend is moving in, and the only other place you can find is an extra $200 a month. Or maybe you suddenly lose your sideline job. Or maybe what happens isn't even terrible: you're asked to be in your best friend's wedding and the costs are up to you to cover!

Financial security isn't just about money. When your budget isn't balanced, neither is your life. Financial wellness leads to mental wellness, which leads to a healthier and more confident and secure individual.

Let's use the aphorism "remember that time is money." You know that feeling when you're late for an audition? You didn't budget enough time, and now, instead of going over your sides one more time or doing your breathing exercises to center yourself, you are crashing into the room sweaty, stressed out, and ill prepared. You are not present. You are not bringing your best self.

Financial stresses will also affect your ability to succeed. If you have not allotted for time delays the morning of an audition, it's going to add a financial burden. Either the train is not stopping at your stop today or your roommate parked their car behind yours and forgot to leave the key. Now the only option is to take a taxi and that costs money. Money you have budgeted for other costs this month. Once you take the taxi, and pay the $20.00, you are already feeling frustrated and uncomfortable. Now, you need to go into an audition, put forth good energy and get a job. The problem is the energy from the financial stress doesn't go away. It comes right in the room with you and subliminally that energy is picked up and can sabotage an opportunity.

No one in this industry is an overnight success. It may take you years to get "discovered," so you must be prepared for a long road. The secret to survival and longevity is financial security. If you do start getting work consistently enough for it to be your only job, you must seek the advice of a financial planner who specializes in creative or nonlinear careers. I have seen too many actors file for bankruptcy a decade or more into their careers. Repeat after me: "I will manage my money and always maintain a balance that covers my consistent monthly expenses and allows for potential business expenses and unexpected opportunities I might want to take advantage of."

The following was designed by Miata Edoga, president and founder of Abundance Bound. Through her work, she helps people develop healthy, compassionate relationships with money. For more information on Edoga and her methods visit AbundanceBound.com and explore the Abundance Bound Financial Empowerment Program, which provides coaching, wisdom, and tools for actors who want to sustain their work in the world without settling for a 9–5 job.

WORKSHEET 4: Run the books

Starting Point: Monthly Profit & Loss

Revenue (gross income)
– Expenses (cost)
_____

Profit or Loss (net income)

Determining Average Monthly Expenses

Using the tool you find most comfortable (app / software, spreadsheet, pen(cil) and paper) . . .

1 Gather 6 months of statements from ALL accounts.
2 Review categories list and cross out any that don't apply.
3 Record the individual amounts spent in each category.
- Start with the first category. Go through all 6 months of statements and record (on a separate sheet) the amount from every time you spent in that category. Cross out the transaction on your statement as you record it.
- Add up the total, write it down, and divide by 6 to calculate the average monthly amount you spent in that category.
- Write that number next to the category name.
- Continue this process until you have a number next to every category you did not cross out.

4 Calculate the total and average for each category.
5 Total all categories to determine your average monthly expenses.

Remember!

- Go through each transaction.
- There are no shortcuts.
- This is the most important work you will do in this process.

Determining Average Monthly Revenue

Non-Industry (past 6 months)

1 Cross out any categories that don't apply.
2 Review bank statements and/or check stubs.
3 Calculate total earned per source.
4 Divide by 6.
5 Record average monthly amount per source.

Industry (past 5 years)

- Review tax returns and/or bank statements.
- Record total industry earnings for each year.

Categories & Expenses List

These categories and expenses are suggestions. You should feel free to personalize and/or add titles as makes sense for you.

Business Costs:

Accompanist	$	Parking / Tolls (Business)	$
Accountant/ Bookkeeper	$	Passport	$
Attorney/ Legal Fees	$	Photo Shoot / Reproduction / Lithos	$
Books/ Scripts/ Music	$	PO Box / Safe Deposit/ Storage	$
Business Bank Fees	$	Professional Registries	$
Business Interest	$	Casting	$
Business Cards / Stationery/ Postcards	$	Props	$
Business Gifts	$	Publicist	$
Business License	$	Business License	$
Commissions (Agent)	$	Rental Theatre Space / Rehearsal Hall	$
Commissions (Manager)	$	Resume Service & Reproduction	$
Costume Repair /Cleaning/ Maintenance	$	Sides	$
Demo (Audio, Video)	$	Software	$
Dining (Business)	$	Travel (Business)	$
Dues (Unions/ Professional Societies)	$	Uniforms /Professional Costumes	$
Equipment (Purchase / Rental)	$	Web Site/Domain Web Hosting	$
Equipment (Maintenance)	$	_____	$
Graphic Design	$	_____	$
Instrument Tuning	$	**TOTAL = $**	

Debt:

Credit Card Minimum 1	$	Taxes	$
Credit Card Minimum 2	$	_____	$
Credit Card Minimum 3	$	_____	$
Credit Card Minimum 4	$	_____	$
Personal Loans	$		
Second Morgage	$		
Student Loan	$	**TOTAL = $**	

Education/Professional Development

Books/ Scripts	$	Subscriptions (Trade Publications)	$
Classes / Workshops/ Seminars	$	_____	$
Coaching	$	_____	$
Research (Tickets, Movies, etc.)	$	_____	$
School Tuition	$	**TOTAL = $**	

Food

Coffee	$	_____	$
Dining Out	$	_____	$
Groceries	$	_____	$
Snacks	$		
Takeout Delivery	$	**TOTAL = $**	

Health/Beauty

Acupuncture/ Chiropractor	$	Prescriptions	$
Beauty	$	Psychotherapy	$
Dental	$	Vitamins/ Supplements	$
Fitness	$	_____	$
Massage	$	_____	$
Medical Bills	$	_____	$
Personal Growth	$		
Physical Therapy	$	**TOTAL = $**	

Insurance

Earthquake	$	Umbrella	$
Homeowner	$	_____	$
Life	$	_____	$
Medical	$	_____	$
Renters	$	**TOTAL = $**	

Living

Alimony / Child Support	$	Housekeeping / Laundry	$
Amazon	$	Netflix/ Hulu	$
Babysitting	$	Pets	$
Bank Fees	$	Property Tax	$
Cash	$	Rent/ Mortgage/ Condo Fees	$
Clothing	$	Storage	$
Entertainment / Recreation	$	_____	$
Furniture/ Appliances	$	_____	$
Gardener	$	_____	$
Gifts	$		
Household Repairs/ Maintenence	$	**TOTAL = $**	

Office Expense

Batteries	$	Printer Supplies (Ink, paper, Toner, etc.)	$
Copy Service	$	_____	$
Fax Service	$	_____	$
Office Supplies	$	_____	$
Postage / Courier	$	**TOTAL = $**	

Telephone / Utilities

Burglar Alarm	$	Phone (Landline)	$
Cable/ Satellite	$	Voicemail	$
Cell Phone	$	Water / Sewer / Garbage	$
Electric	$	_____	$
Fax	$	_____	$
Gas Bills	$	_____	$
Internet	$	**TOTAL = $**	

Transportation

Bus/ Subway	$	Repair	$
Car Loan/ Lease	$	Taxi / Car Service	$
Gasoline	$	_____	$
Insurance	$	_____	$
Parking/ Tolls	$	_____	$
		TOTAL = $	

Travel

Airfare	$	_____	$
Lodging	$	_____	$
Transportation (Car Rental, Taxi, Bus, Parking, Tolls, etc.)	$	_____	$
		TOTAL = $	

Wealth Building

Savings / Investments $ Donations/Charitable Giving $
                                      TOTAL = $

Revenue Worksheet

Use this worksheet to compute your average current monthly income.

Feel free to personalize and/or add titles as makes sense for you.

Non-Industry Income (past 6+ months)

Sideline Employment Source 1	$
Sideline Employment Source 2	$
Unemployment Insurance Benefits	$
Residuals / Royalties	$
Food Stamps / SNAP	$
Public Assistance	$
State Disability	$
Social Security/ SSD	$
Supplemental Security Income	$
Pension	$
Worker's Compensation	$
Alimony / Child Support (Received)	$
Spouse / Family Support	$
Interest / Investment Income	$
Other	$
Other	$
Other	$

Average Total Monthly Income = $

Industry (past 5 years)

Year 1:	$
Year 2:	$
Year 3:	$
Year 4:	$
Year 5:	$

Create a timeline for your goals

Now that you know how much money is coming in and going out, you can use that information to figure out which projects and opportunities to pursue and when to do that.

A short-term opportunity might be a class you just heard about that's being offered as a "one-time-only" thing. Say a showrunner is teaching a workshop for actors who want to learn to write for TV—which is exactly one of your long-term goals. The class is in three months and you don't have $300. Fortunately, though, you have an extensive and accurate assessment of your financials. In other words, you go talk to your CFO to figure out how to get the $300, either by reallocating current expenses, or picking up more shifts.

A long-term project might be a script you want to write. Scripts take time and again, time is money. So you'll need to sit with your CFO to figure out how much time you can allocate per week to this new, ongoing endeavor that won't bring in cash.

Notice that I didn't say your script "won't bring in cash yet" — the truth is that it might never bring in cash, and further, that is OK. If you fall into the trap of thinking that you will sell the script someday, and that cash will come in then, you will be more likely to build up a little debt now. This is how the debt cycle starts. This is the beginning of the demise of your career. You have to work under the assumption that this script will never bring in money. If it ever does, then great, you got a windfall. I want you to bet on yourself creatively but don't gamble financially.

Only consider the money that's coming in and going out now. Apply risk-versus-reward thinking to every purchase. For example, are the fancy $1000 headshots really worth the extra shifts you'll have to pick up to pay for them? Or are the $500 headshots good enough even though they are not from a hyped photographer? Remember, you only need to start with two to three poses. Out of the hundreds of proofs, there are always usable photos. Remember that headshots are not the only images out there: Instagram, websites, LinkedIn, etc. can all help in presenting your image. Plus, you're going to need new headshots every five years or so. It's an ongoing expense, so try to find a reasonable way to manage it. It's not just about headshots. It's always a risk/reward proposition.

Several seats at your board table will help weigh in on this kind of decision making process, including your CEO, CFO, and Head of Creative Development.

Everything you want to do and achieve requires resources. The CFO can help you strategize and prioritize. The CFO can sit down with you and help you save for the things you want. But it takes communication. It takes strategy. Finances are like a game of chess. Every move triggers a chain of events, has possible consequences or advantages, and affects the overall outcome. Make moves thoughtfully and carefully and you'll avoid the anxiety and shame that result from finances being a mess. Most important, when your finances are in order, you won't have to give up your dreams of being an actor, as you would if you wake up in five years with $30,000 in credit card debt. Do not skip the following, life-changing interview with financial wellness expert Rebecca Selkowe.

Interview about financial wellness with Rebecca Eve Selkowe, a NYC-based Accredited Financial Counselor®, attorney, and musician. Selkowe has a private financial coaching practice and runs the financial wellness program at a non-profit that serves professionals in the entertainment industry.

Wendy: What are some of the biggest challenges when working with creative artists?

Rebecca: "The system" is set up for one job with one W2, not for performing artists with insufficient, inconsistent, and multiple streams of income. Most of the mainstream advice about managing cash flow and budgeting is useless to artists. But it is absolutely possible, and even essential, to have systems in place as a creative person — it is just a lot more work, and many artists find it daunting even to begin. I try to help them see that, as my flute teacher would say, "It's not hard—it's just new."

The other main challenge is navigating the inner-game piece, what they think and feel about themselves or their situation. Why can't this be easier? Why do I have to work so hard to make this work? Why don't I feel like a grown up yet? The practical aspects of money management — which, again, are more daunting than actually difficult — can be a challenge when these very real emotions get in the way.

Finally, I think there is an element of resistance that pops up because of a very real fear of what they'll find when they look at their numbers. Either because they don't want to be boxed in and have to "stick" to anything, or because they'll discover that their "crazy" career choice is completely impractical and they'll have to give it up and get a boring office job just like their family says. Or both.

W: How do you break down your objectives into a tool kit?

R: The first step is to learn as much as you can about the basics of budgeting, debt, and savings. Read. Take classes.

The next step is to get as clear as possible on what you want. So often we ignore this piece and try to focus on solutions without really taking a step back to ask, Why do I care? What do I hope to get out of this?

Third: gathering, organizing, and analyzing information about where you are now. On a basic level you must know very detailed information about what is coming in, what is going out, what you own, and what you owe.

Fourth: plan. Take all the information you've gathered and analyzed, and all the soul-searching you've done to determine what you want, and put it together into a plan that feels right and reasonable.

Finally, implement that plan. As you do, keep gathering information and asking yourself what you want and what you need in order to keep moving forward. Get support! Do you need to call the friend who will hold your hand, or the one who will kick your ass? Practice asking for what you need. And keep learning and educating yourself along the way.

W: Is there a correlation between financial wellness and success?

R: Yes! The state of our finances can wreak major havoc on our physical health (stress). There's an element of desperation that fades when you feel more in control of your finances that will help you get more of what you want. Being at an audition screaming to yourself, "I HAVE TO BOOK THIS SO I CAN PAY MY RENT!" will absolutely steal focus away from your work. And of course, the more control you have over your financial situation, the more freedom you have to pursue the projects that really mean something to you.

W: How do you feel about credit cards?

R: Credit cards are a way to establish credit. If you have no history of credit, you'll be considered risky when you need a loan. So I am definitely pro credit cards. It's credit-card debt that becomes problematic. The best way to use a credit card is only to charge in a month what you can pay back in a month, because debt can get very expensive, very quickly. This rule is not always practical or easy to follow for performing artists whose income fluctuates from month to month. Borrowing and paying back only the minimum can feel like the best and only option. So if you do that, it is important to stay vigilant about your debt and understand that carrying a balance on a credit card literally comes at a price.

Carrying too much debt for too long eventually begins to interfere with your ability to focus and show up as your best self in auditions and performances. I never want my clients to be in a position to have to stop acting, even if temporarily, to focus on their debt, but this is an unfortunate reality for some.

The truth is, as with any business, you often have to spend money to make money as an actor. The options and opportunities for spending this money can seem endless. Whenever possible, try to look at acting expenses as investments, and do a one-for-one to determine whether you are getting a good return. What this can look like: I want to take this class, it costs this much, how am I going to make that back? When determining whether to pay for something now using a credit card, or to wait and save up for it, you can ask yourself, "Is it really true that this is a one-time thing, and there won't be another opportunity like this?" Or, "Do I have to put this on a credit card and pay a ton of interest, or does it make more sense to wait and save up for the next one?"

W: If you have a hyphenate talent that has potential to be a lucrative side business, something that you can control and filter in as you need it, should you open a separate business account?

R: You don't necessarily need an LLC or Corporation right off the bat, but at least start practicing like you have one. Open a separate bank account, whether it's a second personal checking account or a business checking with an Employer ID Number (EIN). So you have your personal checking and, say, your photography-income checking. That way, you are treating it like it is a business. You can pay yourself a "salary" out of the money you earn in your photography account. If you need to make an investment in, say, new equipment, and you haven't earned enough yet in your photography account to pay for it, you can loan your photography account money from your personal account. It is mostly about keeping good records and can be as simple as making a transfer that at some point you will pay back. This transferring back and forth may seem silly, but this is what businesses do!

W: When you launch out as a well trained actor, the idea of Plan B can feel immediately like a defeat. How much should actors be encouraged to really, alongside Plan A, develop Plan B?

R: I think we can totally re-frame this!I It is not "Plan B" — a second choice. It doesn't have to be an either-or. If, say, you have a second job as a tax preparer, that tax preparer job allows you to be an actor. Your tax preparation clients are financing your acting career as opposed to your credit card company financing your acting career.

There are (many) times when art doesn't bring in income. During the times art isn't resulting in income, something else has to, because the bills and expenses will keep coming. It can be very challenging to accept this. You have to realize that there is nothing wrong with you as a performing artist if you're not generating income yet.

W: You sit down all the time with creatives in different phases of this financial journey. What is the worst thing you see?

R: Massive credit card debt, and being too terrified and/or overwhelmed to stare it down. It always comes back to debt! Certain levels of debt are manageable for most working actors. It is possible to carry and repay $5,000 or even $10,000 worth of debt through carefully reducing expenses and finding sure ways to increase income. But when the debt, especially credit card debt, creeps into the multiple five-figure range, just the interest piling up on that debt makes the math stop working. At that point, full repayment may not be possible and we need to start at least exploring the idea of bankruptcy, or some other form of debt relief.

This is not a judgment, but rather an unfortunate reality. Using credit cards to float you for a few months can make sense if you factor in the interest charges and have a plan to pay them all off when the money comes in. But that's not what usually happens. The amount of interest credit card issuers charge is absolutely horrifying. If you can find a way to keep money flowing in so that you don't have to rely on credit cards, you will give yourself a much better financial foundation.

And the artists who are realistic about it are the ones who are successful. I have many clients who are on the precipice of having to make the decision to do their Plan B and only their Plan B because they have gotten themselves into an untenable position financially.

W: What age is that person usually?

R: Their 30s. Early to mid 30s.

W: So it's a ten-year period, from the time they leave these programs?

R: Yes. For many, debt builds up slowly over time. If you're borrowing $200 more than you can afford to pay back each month, that's $2,400, plus possibly another $300 in interest in the first year. That level of debt is manageable. But if the $200 monthly deficit continues, after 10 years now we have closer to $30,000, which is much harder to manage.

Facing our finances, particularly when we feel like we've done things wrong, can be an intensely emotional experience. Even when prompted to look forward, many of my clients want to rehash the past and what they see as their past mistakes. They are so mad at themselves and so ashamed and beating themselves up. Instead, I'm picturing these parallel tracks of them doing Plan A and Plan B the whole time, so there is never a time when they have to choose the latter.

W: Plan B is not a bad word. It stands for a Plan Badass. You're going to develop another piece of yourself, which is exciting.

R: Yes! Financial wellness is not for the faint of heart. Building habits takes time; breaking old ones and creating new ones takes even longer. We have to spend time "sitting in the muck," as one of my clients put it. And "looking at it with the house lights on," in the words of another. It takes time and practice, and this is a journey. Those who are willing to be vulnerable, who put in the work, seek support, show up, face the proverbial music and take ownership and control of their situation, are the ones who six months, a year later, two years later, find that the universe has provided for them. Having systems set up means you can proactively seek out opportunities and be ready when they come, rather than reacting to the next crisis.

Choosing sideline jobs strategically

You are an actor. That means you live in a "gig" economy. When you are able to make money from your art, it is a joyful and positive affirmation that you are where you are supposed to be. However, there will be down-time and gaps in between jobs. While you're auditioning, waiting to get that job … you'll have to bring cash in from somewhere else.

There are several things to consider when choosing a sideline job. Do you need your days open for auditions or your nights open for standup shows? Do you want a job with flexible or regular hours? Do you want to have the opportunity to swap shifts with other employees at the last minute if needed? These are important considerations. I have another thing for you to consider: pursue a sideline job that will give you meaningful work.

For example, there are three different tiers of side jobs. The bottom tier is anything you do for quick and expendable income. Basically, gig work. Like Taskrabbitt, Doordash or Uber. The middle tier is when you turn your specific skills and talents into higher profile work that pays better and is more fulfilling. The top tier is when you turn those skills and talents into a business.

My challenge to all artists — or anyone considering an entrepreneurial endeavor — is to ask what skills and talents are already in your wheelhouse, and then lean into them. For example, if you double majored in French, consider becoming a French tutor. If you are very good with children, instead of nannying or babysitting, you could be a crafts teacher or camp counselor. And if it goes well, maybe you throw together a proposal and launch your own after-school arts program. How about coaching younger actors? Use the skills and knowledge you've acquired through training and apply it to a younger demographic. What if you had help from a recent college BFA as you were thinking of this as a career or even just making choices for your college auditions? I remember when I started teaching and I was concerned that I wasn't credentialed enough, but a colleague assured me that I knew "way more than I thought and just sharing that knowledge was invaluable." It's not a stretch to look for sideline jobs that pay more than minimum wage and bring you a stronger sense of accomplishment.

At the start of your career, you'll spend more time at your sideline job than you will spend acting. I suggest the higher tier jobs because they will be more fulfilling and can make you feel creative and in control. You don't have to struggle to be an artist. Merge a side job with a skill you already possess and you'll be more likely to make connections you care about. It's a related conversation.

Don't fear opportunity, a case study

A former student of mine is a good photographer. Friends started asking her to do their headshots. Eventually, she was asked to shoot a wedding. She called me with concerns. She was afraid that if she started a business as a photographer, she would stop being an actor.

That's just fear talking. I told her she should absolutely open a photography business. She gets to decide how much time to devote to it. She gets to decide whether that's her main job or her side job. Additionally, she will meet actors and fellow creatives along the way which will lead to more contacts for her personal or professional database.

There doesn't need to be fear or shame in a side job — first and foremost because work begets work and it's only shameful if the work you chose is not realistically supporting you. But also, I hear you: you're afraid your sideline job will define you, or eclipse your acting pursuits. Nope. You get to define how you are defined. And you will never ever be defined as an actor if you can't afford to continue pursuing it.

Closing thoughts

Finances are not emotional. There is nothing ambiguous about financial responsibility. An account balance must be maintained. Ordered finances are the number-one sign of a healthy company. Speaking of that, let's now reach across the table to shake the hand of your Head of HR.

4

Head of Human Resources

The Head of HR is in charge of keeping your company of sound body and mind — literally. Think of it as macro self care. So, how do you ensure you are a happy and high functioning employee? Let's take components from the traditional framework and apply it to the life of an actor.

In order to maintain mindset and health, the Head of HR has five main duties:

- **Manage healthcare.** Research to find the best plan and stay on top of the paperwork.
- **Stay physically healthy.** This also includes nutrition and, to please your CFO, meal planning.
- **Maintain mental health.** When it feels like this industry is beating you up, you'll have ways to remember who you are.
- **Secure a mentor and support network.** You'll have questions even this book can't answer.
- **Establish and uphold a personal Bill of Rights.** You need to be clear about your boundaries.

This is a pivotal position. It's pivotal in the sense that the Head of HR must constantly check in to ensure that the plans enacted to maintain physical and mental well-being are still working. If not, the long-term effectiveness of your company will be compromised. In other words, the Head of HR is the barometer of what works for you and of what needs reassessing or fine tuning. Let's dig in!

Manage healthcare

As an actor, you are your body. Your instrument is your business. No one in any other business would fail to have their assets insured. You must have a healthcare plan. Whether it's through a job, purchased independently, or through a union, all performing artists need coverage. Your CFO will tell you that this is an expense that must be budgeted and maintained. And if you're planning to stay on your parents' plan for as long as you can, you need to be budgeting to cover the future expenses when you age out. The deductible you choose is entirely up to you.

My other directive around healthcare is to be communicative about the parameters of any health issue you may be having. Don't assume that such issues will negatively impact your opportunities. However, that will definitely happen if you don't share your issues with relevant partners and mentors. You need to be upfront with any issues you have so that teams can plan accordingly around your needs.

Failure to communicate, a case study

A lot of actors don't want to share such issues because they don't want to seem unavailable. But not communicating can create a big mess for yourself. I had a kid in my class who severely tore his ACL and wound up going through multiple surgeries. He missed several classes, as well as opportunities to interface with people in the industry. He was completely waylaid by the injury and didn't communicate that properly to the people who needed to know. Worse, I assumed he wasn't showing up because he didn't care and was unreliable. That compromised my trust. I certainly didn't plan to talk him up to colleagues or advocate for him to get opportunities. Of course, once I learned what was going on, my opinion changed—which is why communicating from the start is so important.

If he had shared that he wasn't available for rehearsals and auditions because he was dealing with a healthcare directive, not only would I have trusted him, but also he and I and his partners could've developed a contingency plan to better use this time. If you've torn an ACL, you won't be going out for westerns or jobs where you're playing a football player. But you can go out for other jobs! So you need to know the timeline for your rehab schedule and effectively communicate that.

Stay physically healthy

This is a grueling, demanding business. If you're going to sustain yourself, you must be healthy. It's not about being any specific body type, it's about how you feel. When you walk into an audition, do you want to be sluggish and cloudy or alert and optimistic? Again, your body is your business. It is imperative to implement a fitness regimen of some kind. It doesn't mean hours at a gym or expensive classes. It means doing anything that can get your body moving and staying fit and flexible. Take a walk and listen to podcasts that interest you. Later you can share that information with others. Some of my students participate in activities that might also lead to acting work, for example dance or martial arts. Many of my students take classes in the Alexander Technique, yoga, or anything that strengthens mind-body awareness, since acting requires a strong connection to the body. The most important thing is to find a form of fitness that is sustainable.

The other part of taking care of our bodies is directly linked to nutrition. Not eating or lack of meal prep is a huge form of self-sabotage. This seems like common sense — and it is! — yet my students fall into this trap constantly. Don't be in a place where you're running around to auditions and haven't eaten properly. If you get low blood sugar, or are in a carb coma, you can have headaches or dizziness, or have your focus compromised in any number of ways. Plus, you don't know how long the wait will be and the longer you wait without nutrition, the more you're not present in the room. And your CFO will tell you that pulling the car over for a $20 salad is not an option either (there's that extra $20 again!).

Plan out your meals so you're not forced to grab something expensive or non-nutritious. Eat breakfast, keep nuts in your car or backpack. Consider packing some kind of snack bag (hummus and veggies or something) every morning, in case you get a last-minute call for an audition at any point during the day.

Your body is your creative instrument. Make sure it is tuned every time you walk into an audition room.

Maintain mental health

Mental wellness is paramount to your company. HR can't have effective employees, stand behind their work, or manage disputes effectively if the members of the organization are not self-aware, mindful individuals. Companies spend millions of dollars to create better leaders and communicators among their employees. Fortunately, you only have to look out for you.

First, I want to tell you about a specific kind of therapy that many of my students have connected with (and which helps them handle the bumps in the road and stay on course). You may have already heard about Dialectical Behavioral Therapy (DBT) or Cognitive Behavioral Therapy (CBT). I've had guests come in to teach this methodology at my seminars and it's literally changed lives. I was so thrilled to have connected my students with a resource that works. I want to do the same for you. Here, I will share a few tenets of DBT that resonate with my work and those that apply to the life of an actor. (Seek out more information on both of these types of therapy to get the full picture.)

"The stories we tell ourselves" — about why we did or didn't get an audition, for example — are some of the biggest obstacles actors face. Think about when you're in the waiting room for an audition, and you hear the whole room laughing on the other side of the wall. An actor walks out of the room, and the casting director gives them a big hug. You think, "Shit, that's it. They just got the role. Why am I sitting here?" You build a story in your head that has absolutely no bearing in reality. Maybe that actor got a hug because they and the casting director have mutual friends or they are reconnecting after running into each other. The point is, you have no idea and, nevertheless, you created a lot of bad stress for yourself right before an audition. Another reasonable stressor is putting self tape out "into the void." Many actors will tape repeatedly and receive little to no feedback. They put work and time into an audition with no way of knowing whether it was viewed favorably or not. This opens up a lot of self talk and examination and starts dialogue that questions the essence of you, from your looks to your talent. How do you navigate these situations and give yourself a method in which to regulate anxieties?

In between the reasonable mind and the emotional mind, is the wise mind. Your reasonable mind approaches things analytically and intellectually. Your emotional mind tends to think more erratically. The goal is to get to a place where you can observe your behavior and say, "I don't want to live in either of those dualities. I want to live in the center, in the wise mind." DBT and CBT promote the wise mind. "Schemas" is a psychological term for patterns of thought or behavior that people use to process information. There can be a cycle of negative or false beliefs that disempower us over time. Learning a new way to frame and cognitively face these beliefs gives us renewed focus and options. Looking at those various extenuating circumstances and options with a wise mind allows for growth.

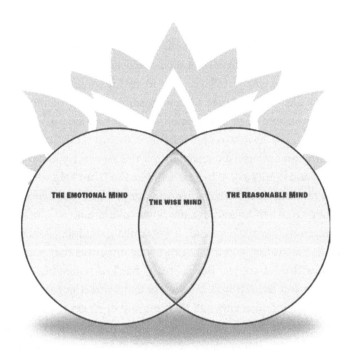

The wise mind

Remove judgment words—"this always happens to me," "I'll never get a break"—from your language. Remind yourself that the "stories we tell" are not necessarily true. When you do, you free yourself from catastrophizing and can then focus that energy in positive ways, for example nailing the audition regardless of the actor who went in before you . . . or the lack of feedback in the room . . . or the amount of time they gave you.

There's so much you can't control in this industry. But you can control the stories you tell yourself, how you're going to respond to a situation, and how you're going to show up. DBT helps you get unstuck from conflict within yourself or with others because it expands your way of seeing things. It helps you look for what's left out of your understanding of the situation and it lets go of that black-and-white way of thinking, the all-or-nothing way of seeing a situation, which actors have a tendency to do. Actors get emotional about things — being emotional is what makes them good at acting! — which can lead to negative behaviors. Don't let those behaviors dictate or sabotage what you really want.

Practically speaking, DBT can also help guide you toward healthy decision making. Consider this common scenario: you arrive for an 11am audition, but they're running behind. Now it's 11:30, and the two people signed in before you haven't gone in either. You're starting to feel stress. You came in fresh and ready to perform, but no longer have the same energy and enthusiasm. You're also anxious because you don't know why it's taking so long or what the next hour will look like. Then, you see what we just discussed: an actor comes out and gives everyone big hugs. Throw another stressor on the pile.

At this point, you have two choices: find a way to return to equilibrium and feel fresh and enthusiastic again, or tell the assistant you have another appointment and kindly ask to be rescheduled. DBT can help you make that decision by teaching you to recognize and assess stress identifiers, so you'll know, as they say, when to hold 'em and when to fold 'em.

Now: rejection. It's not personal. If you don't get a job, it's not because you're bad. It means that you did not meet the directives they were looking for. You know this, of course. But it's really hard to remember that in the moment when you feel rejected. I don't like that word. The goal is to get the job. People go on job interviews all the time and don't get the job. It doesn't mean they were rejected. It simply means there was another candidate for the job that felt like a better choice at that time. As actors, it feels personal and acting is highly personal. After all, "they saw my work and don't want me" seems like it could translate to "they saw my work and don't like me." We have to re-frame that conversation. Again, DBT can help. We can say "they don't like me for THIS role, they don't want me THIS time and there will be a next time because the win was getting called in to begin with!"

The other seemingly simple way to re-frame "rejection"—although of course it takes practice— is to change your expectations. First of all, even if you don't book the job, every audition is a step toward booking a job down the line. But I want you to think bigger: what if an audition is not first and foremost about booking a job at all? What if you view it as an opportunity to engage in your art form or to have a casting office learn your work as an actor? You chose this profession because you love to act. Every audition is an opportunity to create character and be in your body, a chance to do what you love.

At this point in your career, you'll spend more time in auditions than you will actually working. The audition should be the most coveted, wonderful experience because for those five minutes you're doing exactly what you're dedicating your life to. Make sure you're finding a way to make auditions as artistically fulfilling as possible. Do your best to cut out the noise of competition and judgment, so auditioning can be about the joy of acting. Train yourself to embrace those incremental joys, or you'll never be satisfied. Beware of what can also be described as "toxic positivity." This is when fellow creatives minimize or mask their true feelings about a stressful or overwhelming situation. Everyone uses different coping mechanisms. Use real talk to help you cope and don't fall for what appearances show on the outside. Go forward with the purpose you were intended to fulfill. Let that be your only objective.

I was floored, while listening to the Smartless podcast (episode 26), and heard Bryan Cranston say, "I kept going into an audition thinking I was there to get a job and then I finally realized, 'Oh, this is the wrong way to go in.' You have to go in to do a job, not get a job. So if you walk into an office and you don't want anything from them—you're there to give them something—your energy completely changes. You came in with confidence and you leave them with your work." That's exactly how it should go every time.

Look, DBT or CBT may not necessarily be the path for you. The point is to find a method that supports and sustains mental wellness. Bombing auditions, getting called back five times and still not getting the part, or getting a job and then losing it: this is all commonplace. It's the nature of the business you've chosen. And you may not get a lot of feedback. You may never know why. You may only hear, "We went in another direction" or "Not right for the role." Find a way to exercise whatever mental gymnastics are necessary to enable you to pick yourself up and keep going. This industry isn't for the thin skinned, so find a way to get out of an emotional state and into a wise state.

For more comprehensive study on CBT and DBT, please find a practitioner who specializes in this therapy and follow the links to the online resources for worksheets from Therapist Aid. I would suggest focusing on the following worksheets in the DBT section labeled:

Distress Tolerance Skills
Emotional Regulation
Interpersonal Effectiveness
ACCEPTS

These resources will challenge and help reframe destructive or negative thoughts. Use them as a check-in before/after an emotionally charged event to unpack the experience and gain insight into your reactions or assumptions.

Secure a mentor and support network

No actor can handle the stressors of this industry alone. You will need support — specifically from people who personally understand what you're going through. There are two groups in this support network: mentors in the form of industry professionals, and a personal posse made up of your peers.

You will need answers to questions that aren't in any how-to-be-an-actor manuals, not even this one. You'll have a question about a confusing clause in a contract. You'll receive a vague breakdown and feel unsure about how to dress for the audition. You won't know how soon to follow up with an agent because of some specific mitigating circumstances. Don't just guess. Reach out to a former professor, perhaps, or a current acting coach. Maybe you really bonded with a guest artist who did a residence program at your school, or a contact you made during a summer internship. Perhaps the Entertainment Community Fund or the SAG/AFTRA Foundation could point you to resources that will educate you. Don't be shy to lean on any and all resources available.

And if they don't wind up being helpful? Persist. Professors and professionals are busy. If they don't respond right away to your email, that doesn't mean they don't want to—remember DBT!—so it's okay to follow up. Whether or not you hear back after the second attempt, go ahead and ask someone else, too. The point is: be proactive and resourceful.

I had a former student reach out to me saying she didn't know where else to turn. She needed help deciphering a certain piece of a contract. She was still in her BFA program, and had reached out to all the departments, and several specific professors, and no one could give her the information she needed. Yes, that's frustrating. It's your school's job to help you find answers to any question, regardless of whether or not they already know it.

I have two pieces of advice here. First, she was wise to email me. Keep a list of every professional who visits your school. Feel free to reach out to them. Just say, "I was in your session, your words resonated with me, and I have a question about ..." Second, students get a lot done when they make noise within the confines of their academic programs. You have to say, "I'm in a program here, and I need help getting answers." Band together with other students who have the same demands, and you'll be even stronger. You're part of a demographic of emerging artists, who don't have agents and managers yet. You are currently representing yourself, so you will have a lot of questions.

As for your personal support network — your posse — that part is easy and fun. But it still requires follow up, reaching out, and making yourself vulnerable. When people are going out after a class or workshop, join them ... maybe not every time, because you'll have a lot of other demands on your time ... but do devote some of that time to connections. These are the people whose shoulders you'll cry on, and vice versa. And these are the people you'll write plays and films with! The creatives you start out with in this industry are the people you'll eventually work with. Start developing those relationships now. And be nice to everyone: there's a very good chance that actor you're hanging with will be your PA or director one day!

When you start achieving success, that's when you'll need this posse the most. Fame changes how you're treated and the people who knew you beforehand will be some of the only ones you can trust to keep you grounded and remind you what's important.

Establish and uphold a personal Bill of Rights

The most important thing you can do toward maintaining your sanity in this industry is to establish and uphold what I call a personal Bill of Rights. Actors are rarely in control. This can make them even more susceptible to compromising situations, when they fall into the mindset of thinking, "Well, I guess I just have to go along with this because ..." If you find yourself in an uncomfortable or compromising situation, it is not only OK for you to walk away, it is imperative that you speak out and look for support.

Don't be afraid to voice your concern. If you feel discriminated against or bullied, tell someone you trust. This is another reason why it's so important to have mentors. If you're SAG, the union has your back. If you're not, you need to call a former teacher or any connection who can provide support and who can help you navigate the situation, whether by offering personal advice or blowing a whistle on your behalf.

Actors are a hopeful bunch. They have to be! But it's just as important to tune your spidey senses. A low-stakes example: if you get the feeling that someone in the industry is behaving inappropriately, keep all your correspondence with this person in a professional email account, rather than on social media. That's establishing boundaries. A high-stakes example:

if you're having photographs taken in an isolated spot or with a photographer you don't really know, bring a friend. That's putting safety first.

Many actors are afraid both in academia and in the industry that there will be a silent "black balling" if they don't remain complicit. This is not true. Thankfully, the ongoing imperatives surrounding Diversity, Equity and Inclusion are at the forefront in our industry. With heightened awareness and sensitivity we can all work together to help educate each other. It's possible to engage in difficult conversations and point out insensitive behavior when done with humble inquiry and a charitable approach.

We are all learning to be better and working to educate each other and our fellow creatives. Problems can arise, however, when a person goes around the situation and seeks retribution without making a direct attempt to have a candid conversation or to rectify the problem. That makes all involved feel defensive, exposed, and betrayed. Many casting professionals are working hard to create an inclusive atmosphere. Many professors are learning and training to do the same. Microaggressions may be implicit biases that have remained unchecked or redirected. Work to "call in" those who are perpetuating the old stereotypes and paradigms, instead of "calling them out." They will appreciate and value your input.

When possible, partner with them directly, help them listen and be better. We all need each other.

That said, if there is a continuation of or a consistency to the behavior, then seek out support to handle the next steps. Trust your intuition and know the designated officials who are available to you within your institution and industry.

I'd like to pivot to another topic. My students often ask me about nudity on set. It's not uncommon for actors to see the words "nudity required" in a breakdown, know that nudity is something they are opposed to, but then go ahead and submit themselves anyway. They are either hoping that the part will not wind up requiring nudity or that they will navigate it later. So, they accept the audition from the casting director but afterwards their initial feelings about nudity resurface as something they don't actually want to do. They feel taken advantage of, compromised, and ashamed, which can have lasting, detrimental effects on ambition and motivation.

 Do not put yourself in that situation! If you don't want to be part of something where you expose yourself—and remember that your definition of "tasteful" may be different from someone else's—then establish those boundaries clearly. Let your representation know. Don't go out for an audition thinking that maybe it will work out the way you want it to. If you show up for an audition, the creative team expects you to do what's in the script. Luckily nowadays it's common to have an Intimacy Coordinator on set for scripts that require nudity, love scenes or any other kind of physical contact or touch.

Also, learn to recognize scams. A modeling agency calls because they saw your pictures and really want to sign you. They just need you to pay a $200 producing fee, which they'll use to create your photos. Nope. You don't pay them to market you. You enter into a partnership and if they market you and sell you, then they get a percentage of your work. Same goes for representation: You don't pay for auditions! Anytime anyone asks you for money upfront, and you are not getting a deliverable good such as a class or a service, it's a scam.

Last, make a list of those who have been supportive of you and your journey. Count them as your network of angels. They can advise and offer perspective in situations that are unexpected or confusing. You do not have to navigate these waters alone.

Bottom line: Before you move forward in this industry in any capacity, know your boundaries, establish your personal Bill of Rights, and know who you will call if something goes wrong.

Closing thoughts

Your Head of HR and the various departments within that division keep you safe and supported. And in times of crisis, your head of HR will know where to look. But ideally, you'll never find yourself in dire straits, mentally, physically, or emotionally, because your Head of HR understands the importance of preventative self-care. Be clear on your boundaries (nudity, profanity, travel, or any other specifics) that inform your hire-ability.

What's next? Your vision is clear. Your business is funded. You're healthy and ready to go. Now your Head of Marketing will help you tell the world.

5

Head of Marketing & Branding

There are many ways to book roles. You need to get an audition. And you need to nail the audition. Fortunately, marketing and branding help you achieve both. When you take the time to tell the industry who you are, through social media, headshots, and tape, you come to inherently understand that perspective yourself. And when you know what makes you unique, you can walk into an audition room where there are 15 actors, and you are the 16th, and you won't be intimidated.

Marketing and branding teaches you how to honor what makes you stand out, how to represent it to the world, and how to capitalize on it. Once you are capable of doing that, you are at a point where you're either booking parts or truly understanding that they weren't right for you.

The first thing this Head will do is change your mind about marketing and branding in general. Some actors believe they shouldn't have to worry about this sort of stuff, or even that it's beneath them as artists. Not only is that false, it's counterproductive to their development as artists.

Your job as an actor is to be consciously aware of how you're promoting yourself. You want the industry to see films you've made and photos that depict you in the best light possible. If that content doesn't exist yet, you have to create it. And then you have to make sure all of it is seen. It's a lot of work, but it's really fun. Social media has changed everything, making self-promotion less restricted, more playful, and easier to do. I told you this Head would be your best friend: they would have to be, after how much time you'll spend together!

The duties of the Head of Marketing & Branding can be organized into three sections.

- **Determine your brand.** Understand how the world sees you, use that to develop a type and brand, and then expand that brand to show range.

- **Build your brand and platform.** Create content to support the full range of your brand, and curate this content onto various platforms. (This section covers head shots, resumés, social media, and websites.)
- **Promote your brand and platform.** Maintain your social media and websites with schedules and campaigns, build relationships with your audience, and market yourself through casting sites.

Determine your brand

You know you can play lots of different characters. You're a trained actor, you can rise to any and all challenges.

In the Film and TV world, this mentality won't serve you initially. It is important to focus your work into clear types, and you can develop more than one. The sooner you embrace this, the sooner you'll start booking roles. You won't be typecast forever, but you must start out in a "lane." The industry demands that you make a declarative statement regarding how they can first embrace you. Nothing happens until you start booking roles, and that happens when you know your brand. This section will help you figure out how to do that.

We had a branding consultant come into our class to talk to the kids. She pointed at this one guy and immediately said, "You're the lovable loser." And he was very responsive to that! I wondered if he would get defensive, but instead he was very savvy. He loved the fact that she had given him that tagline. Basically, she branded him. She gave him a branding title, and with it, the permission to go out and play into that. Casting is objective driven. Our job in casting is to appreciate the nuances and other facets of your amazing being and personality. But we have a job to do as well. Our job is to say, "We have this role with specific criteria. We have this actor. Does the actor fit that criteria?" If so, we have the answer and everyone's happy.

I'm looking for something specific when I'm helping to build a character. My job is not to pull out all those nuances and color for you. That's your job. Your brand needs to be a bright blinking marquee light. You must take a stand, own a point of view. Casting directors can lean in and work with that. We will be engaged and intrigued. There's a myth that you have to "get" the role but it's actually the opposite: you have to "lose the role." Every time you walk in, we are rooting for you. It's yours to book or yours to lose. Take the risk, take a stand, be available and vulnerable, and let your unique self shine through.

I sometimes will have my students do the following exercise. It's not the definitive barometer of type but it's thought provoking and fun. Go to people from three different areas of your life: family, friends, and strangers. Walk up and ask, without giving them time to think, "What are five words you would use to describe me?" Your family is going to have five, your friends are going to have a slightly different five, and the complete strangers will potentially have the most revealing five. You take those 15 adjectives and therein lies a window to your brand.

Brand is perception. In the first 10 seconds that I meet you, I form an opinion about you and about your essence. I form some kind of feeling. Google the science of first impressions, it's fascinating. What characteristics stand out? Capable, confident, nice, funny, curious, serious? What does clothing and style tell me about attitude and approach to life? We do this kind of evaluating every day of our lives. The only difference is now, as an actor, you're being asked to turn that into something that is a package, something that is a little bit more quantifiable.

Be open to this self-assessment. To buck the responses and say, "This is not who I am," is not a reflective and open attitude. Lean into the feedback you're getting, find the pieces that resonate, and ride that wave until it gets you work. Meanwhile, develop content that shows you in this light *and* other lights you'd like to be perceived in as well.

Next, how do you actually name your brand? Think about the way films are marketed. You're familiar with the term logline? It's the one-sentence description of the entire thing: plot, characters, emotional tone, all of it. That's what you'll do for yourself, except for actors I call it a *tagline* or *trope*. They exist in TV and Film characters everywhere. Try to keep it to two or three words only. I had a student email me saying that his comedic brand is "the adorable douche bag you almost slap but kiss instead." I told him to make it more concise. Make it a bite instead of a meal. "Lovable bad boy" works. Less is always more.

One way to create these taglines is to borrow another practice from the film-marketing playbook: the "high concept pitch," that clichéd practice of saying "this" meets "that." (For example, *"Guess Who's Coming to Dinner* meets *Stepford Wives"* might describe *Get Out.* This gives you an intrinsic understanding of the film without actually knowing anything about it.)

Now, for your brand tagline, think about having "this" and "that" be slightly contradictory. You can take two contrasting characteristics and use them to create a character type with depth and complexity. Specifically, think about finding the light and the dark. One side of a person is positive and the other side is problematic. Interesting characters are complicated. Thinking this way will help you quickly develop and illustrate a compelling, definable type. Absent-minded professor; Co-dependent pixie dreamgirl; Charismatic shapeshifter; Pragmatic chameleon.

Now think about where this brand lives. The lovable bad boy could live in a variety of worlds. Think about setting and add in characters slightly to the left and right of your specific brand in order to expand on the narrative of your branding. If you're the lovable bad boy, maybe you're also a corporate highroller or an Ivy League athlete, or maybe you're the boy next door who's good with parents. But be wary of over diversifying. Choose only two or three.

Just because you pick the lane of "lovable bad boy" doesn't mean that after you get in the door for that particular role, that others are not going to see you in a different context or that you won't be able to show them that they may think of you for other kinds of roles moving forward. You don't have to worry about making that statement and getting pigeonholed because creative people are looking to create more interesting and rich conversations. This is what casting directors pride themselves on being able to do. Yes, they need to know who's the "lovable bad boy" and audition them for that— but then later, when they get their next project, they'll think, "Who is that guy I brought in last time? It would be so fun to see him play completely against type." You have to put your faith in the fact that just because you have chosen a lane that doesn't mean you're going to have to stay in that lane forever. We can figure out where else and how else to cast you after that introduction.

What's my tagline? a case study

Figuring out all your complexities in one sentence . . . that shouldn't be hard, right? It's excruciating.

For most actors the task of reducing their essence to a tagline or catch phrase to highlight their character type or personality requires a process of self-examination and a willingness to show vulnerability, humor, and truth.

I worked with an actor who had a particular sense of humor, lovability, softness and a way with wording that was provocative. The tagline took a lot of thought and rewrites but what we came up with for them was something metaphorical: "Joey is a squishy fruit, juicy and complex with a slight pit of anxiety in the center." The concept was theirs. Every time they signed an email to me it ended with "Your squishy fruit, Joey (they/them)."

I suggested they use that and expand on it. You can do that too. Metaphor or Analogy . . . try it. It's fun, creative and A LOT more interesting than "the best friend next door." Try bringing in a geographical reference and/or a hobby that also describes you in a poetic way:

Baking/Cooking:
Danny is a sweet and salty cookie with a crunchy exterior and a gooey middle.

Gardening:
Violet's petals open up to the sun and grace us with sunshine on a gloomy day.

WORKSHEET 5: Determining Your Brand

Step 1

Ask three people—a family member, a friend, and a stranger — to share five adjectives that describe you. Ask them to prioritize adjectives that describe your personality and essence, as opposed to your appearance (yes, even strangers will be able to do this!).

Step 2

Now, identify a few professions that people who can be described by those 15 adjectives might occupy. Be as specific as possible. For example, I often get strong, confident, outgoing, and sarcastic. One role I could definitely play is a lawyer—but what kind of lawyer? Maybe a lawyer in finance, entertainment, or media. Or maybe a pro-bono social-justice lawyer in a public defender's office.

Step 3

Next, consider geography. Where would this kind of person working in these kinds of professions live? Do they have more of an East Coast or Midwest sensibility? Are they big-city, urban dwellers or do they have a small-town vibe? To use the example of my own brand, it is definitely urban. I could play a Los Angeles-based talent agent, but I'd be even better suited for a high-powered New York City or maybe a Miami million-dollar real-estate agent.

Step 4

Finally, put all of this together into character type descriptions. For example: I'm the 7-figure lawyer in training OR I am the empathetic champion of the people.

WORKSHEET 6: Finding Your Tagline

Based on the concept of utilizing the light and the dark let's walk through an articulation of your type.

1. What is the light side of your type?

Statement: I am a_____
(Example: Pixie Dream Girl. This character uses her crazy quirky energy to help re-imagine and fill the lives of those around her with an infectious dose of optimism, and child-like playfulness.)

2. Now deconstruct that type and create a more complex character, by adding dark characteristics. These attributes are not as appealing. The energy becomes slightly menacing, unpredictable or erratic and invasive. The dark side doesn't have to be wildly tragic. It can just be your fatal flaw. It's the thing that keeps your character from getting what they want.

I am also
(Example: damaged, co-dependent, obsessed, insecure, stuck in my head.)

3. Put them together.

I am a:
(Example: Manic pixie dream girl.)

4. Expand on that statement by giving examples of where we see these types of characters. What TV shows or films have glorified or featured this type of characters? Do these characters live within a fantasy world, a highly stylized world, a small rural town, or some other kind of universe?

World: I live in
(Example: Los Angeles hipster and yuppie scene, as in *New Girl*;
London model/influencer Juno Temple in *Ted Lasso*; psychological
fantasy, as in *Eternal Sunshine of the Spotless Mind*.)

5. Pay attention to the actors who have played these roles. This
   is an interesting discovery of type and similar sensibility.

Actors: These have played my type
(Example: Zooey Deschanel, Juno Temple, Kate Winslet, and
others.)

Flipping from the light to the dark allows actors to create complex
characters. When you can identify material that will help you
market that complexity, you create an interesting presentation for
other creatives. Casting directors are really good at discerning
those complexities and assigning them to various roles they are
casting. Identifying prototypes can help actors identify and find
themselves in material that is being developed or that already
exists.

WORKSHEET 7: Branding Boxes

In an effort to give you lots of ways to play with brand and type, a student gave me another methodology.

Try creating a box for a character you feel you could play that's already in the media and has a distinct characteristic. Fill that box with the characteristics.

If I go back to the prior examples:

Look at the common adjectives that relate to you and adapt those for your own type/character description. If you're a combo of two or more characters, combine certain characteristics from each to create your own.

It's important to stress that this is not what you admire about them or wish you were, instead look at what you have in common with them and what is true to your personality and values.

Build your brand and platform

A student of mine once said that visiting an Instagram page is like looking inside a refrigerator: You can learn a lot about a person based on what's inside. I love this metaphor! Is there a six pack of beer and leftover pizza, or are there all-natural non-GMO products and hemp juice? Instagram accounts are the headshots of today (yes, you still need traditional headshots). This is good news: It gives you much more control than actors used to have. You get to decide what's on your page, and how it represents you. And you get to show far more versatility than you can on an 8 × 11 glossy.

CREATE a visual conversation with your audience. Use pictures, images, quotes, nature, and political and social causes to let the world know about you as a person, not just an actor.

CURATE. Be selective and artistic in your choices. I always use this analogy: Imagine you are a painter and have been granted your first public showing of your work. You have a beautiful gallery with empty walls to "curate" a show of your best and most accomplished work. Hang the works you are most proud of, work that is beautiful and unique to you.

To be clear, just because you're creating your image, that doesn't make it any less authentic. Often my students express their hesitation and resistance to the perception created online. They feel like posting content about themselves is a demand for attention or a cheapening of their craft. When you're in the role of curator, you're less likely to doubt.

In teaching you how to brand and market yourself, I'm not diminishing or even questioning your ability, your art, or the worthiness of your craft. I'm suggesting that you show all of those things that make you worthy and special. Find out what they are, label them, and let the industry know about them. That isn't corruption, it's just information. When you're in the role of the curator, you can take yourself out of that shameful mindset. No one would call artists shameful for hanging their best works for all to see.

Headshots

The most important thing to remember about headshots — both during the shoot and also when you're choosing shots — is the eyes. People always say that the eyes are the windows to the soul. Yep, that is exactly what we are looking for in a casting office. We want to make a connection with you through your photo. Although this is the number one thing you should consider, by far, it is not all.

Consider consulting a stylist or a friend with an eye for style before you take headshots. If you don't have access to a resource that can help, at least spend a good amount of time investigating your brand, where it exists in current TV and film, and how best to represent it in your own photographs. Don't play it safe. Headshots of you wearing a crew neck T-shirt and smiling doesn't tell me enough about you. It doesn't give me specific information. Figure out the characters you will be playing and how to suggest those characters. If you have film on yourself, share it with the photographer and have a dialogue about the image or the essence that you project.

Your headshots, though basic, should illustrate shades of your brand and type. Aim to walk away with three to four different types that are all true to your brand. For example, if your brand is Jewish NY urban sophisticate, perhaps your three looks could be (1) polished professional (upscale gallery assistant, fashion designer/stylist, or Civil Liberties activist); (2) Young mom/caregiver (volunteer, soccer mom, family caregiver); (3) alter-ego (this is a wild-card picture that captures another side of your artistry: musician, painter, graffiti artist, etc.).

Or conversely, if you play a more edgy character type, maybe you choose to wear a black T-shirt with holes in it, studs in your ears, and dark eyeliner, and stand against a moody background. That will give me a lot more information about your personal brand. Then you can contrast that shot with a second, more commercial look that's maybe less contemporary.

If the session doesn't feel right and/or you're editing or second guessing yourself just to be polite, honor and lean into the discomfort, and be able to articulate what you do and don't want out of the session. You're on the clock with them, and they are expensive! A very good friend of mine who is an actress and a photographer said she always knows when an actor is uncomfortable because they ask questions about the choices during a session instead of stating what feels right and wrong.

Avoiding stereotypes, a case study

"I had a photographer once throw a scarf around my neck and put me in a leaf green cardigan from her closet. I have never owned anything in that color. It isn't the way I dress or representative of anything I would buy. They had heard me say "soccer mom." They were being helpful. But it was on me to articulate to them that I was not comfortable with that look. I could have put more thought into it before the session and had a better result." Honor the way you normally dress and your own sense of style. Bring that to the different characters you play rather than letting others base the look on stereotypes they've seen before.

Be authentic, a case study

There was a great actress who came in on an open call for native and indigenous actors. She had a fabulous sense of personal style: long hair, feather earrings, a long gauze skirt, and a loose earthy top. After her audition I asked, "Why are you using this headshot?" It was a generic and safe photo. Her hair was combed carefully, her outfit looked like a 50's housewife. I said, "You are so fabulous and free, you need to bring that into your headshots." Three months later I got a text and then a call from her. She had taken my advice and was getting called in and had started booking!!

As a young actor, you haven't had as much time to inherently understand your brand and how to articulate it. But the more you can wrestle those questions to the ground and understand the images that will best reflect you, the more productive and helpful every photo shoot will be. Doing so will also help you dress for auditions ... and meetings ... and mixers. The more you understand the intersection of you and your brand, the better able you will be to represent yourself to the industry.

Resumés

Here are the golden rules when it comes to a resumé.

1 One page only.
2 Take off your high school credits.

3   Get a Google Voice number. This free service will not only provide you with a business number, but also transcribes all voicemails and send them over email, so you can easily access your messages while otherwise engaged.

4   Don't put a physical address on your resumé.

5   If you want to use a thumbnail photo of another look (different from your headshot) on your resumé, that's fine. It's also helpful if for any reason you bring a physical copy into the room and your picture gets separated from your resumé.

6   Special skills: These are skills that enhance your hire ability. They are called special skills for a reason. You need to be proficient and at an expert level, and able to put them into action in the room, unless of course it's horseback riding. In other words, this is not something you would have to train to get better at. This is something you could immediately perform or do, and the production could count on a strong level of proficiency.

7   There's no need to label your college work as "student" or "thesis" films. Name the producer or director in the same way you would for an independent film. I am not suggesting that you lie on your resumé. I do think that if you have been on a set, have had a lead role in a film, have worked with a producer and director, that piece of work is substantial and important, regardless of whether it was a student or independent film. Once you graduate, there is little distinction between the two. A piece of independent film is a piece of independent film. Don't let semantics define your experience. Industry professionals want to see that you have knowledge and a comfort level on set.

8   Other thoughts regarding your resume:

Awards: you can make a small note with an asterisk and include the award in smaller text under the block of credits in that section.

Training: List teachers that are relevent to your training especially if they are of note to other industry professionals. If you think they are strong points for your resume, include them. If there's additional space in your Actors Access account, use that to list other/additional teachers and training.

Height/Weight: As a rule , this is more of a commercial imperitive. If asked, you can address your height in the auditon slate. Weight is not appropriate.

There is a section called "size card" on Actors Access and in "sizes" on Casting Networks. Fill these out if you choose.

Jane Smith

(555) 123-4567
janesmithactor@gmail.com
www.janesmithactor.com/@janesmithactor

THEATER

The Wolves	#7	Goodman Theatre/Sophia Stallings, Dir.
Witch	Winnifred	Geffen Playhouse/Alex Medina, Dir.
Anything Goes	Ensemble	Paper Mill Playhouse/Bisbee Hall, Dir.
Rapture, Blister, Burn**	Avery	Williamstown/Amy Lin, Dir.
** Reading		

XXXXUNIVERSITY

The Seagull	Nina	Carole James, Dir.
Romeo and Juliet	Lady Capulet	Annie Taylor, Dir.
Gruesome Playground Injuries	Kayleen	Ryan Glass, Dir.
Company	Marta	Laurie Grant, Dir

FILM/TV

The Long Road	Lead	Alexandra Wolf, Dir.
It's All Fixed	Lead	Will Hayes, Dir.
Maybe Someday	Supporting	Lily Connor, Dir

EDUCATION/TRAINING

XXXX University BFA Acting (2021)

Acting	Rachel Benjamin, Suzanne McDonald, Robert Silver, Oliver Ortega
Voice/Speech	Stephen Jones, Bonnie Majors
Movement	Elizabeth Davis, Catherine Edwards

Royal Academy of Dramatic Arts, London Study Abroad

The Groundlings: Intermediate Improv

Howard Fine Acting Studio: Ongoing Scene Study

SV Voice Studio: Ongoing Voice Lessons

SKILLS: Spanish (Proficient); Certified Pilates Instructor; Singer (Alto); Dance (Tap/Ballet/Jazz); Ukulele; Piano; Accents/Dialects: Western Ireland, Dublin, British RP, New York; Impressions upon request; Indoor Cycling; Knitting

Content for social media

Beyond headshots, also take photos and videos—or create any piece of material—that helps depict your brand. Say to the industry, "Here are the different ways to cast me," and put those materials on the walls of your social-media galleries. Keep your personal account separate from your professional account. When you do create an account, use the bio to describe your type succinctly and with humor. It's an opportunity for a memorable branding bite. For example, here are some Instagram bios of actors I've worked with.

One actress is a self-described "old Jewish woman living in a young body." Her Instagram bio reads:

Actor & Writer
Bagel Enthusiast
Jewish Mom Friend

[then her reps, a link to an article she wrote, and her website]

This young Black actress infuses her Baltimore upbringing into roles that are timeless, contemporary, and fierce. Her instagram bio reads:

If Taraji P. and Kerry W. had a love child
BADA (Yale School of Drama) Alumn
Pace U Alumn

[then a film credit with a link]

This young comedic actor infuses a messy, unapologetic struggle with a take-charge attitude. His Instagram bio opens with:
    My name is _____, non-union, living at home, and I'll be reading for the part of "broke college grad."

Initially, It's not about getting followers, it's about sharing something that doesn't feel like a "have to," but a "want to," and if it's bringing you joy and creating conversation, then it will find its audience. Social media provides an opportunity to create a window into you and your business life. Any short videos or images that represent your work and who you are as an actor will become clues for detective casting directors.

Next, show your brand immersed in the parts of life that you appreciate (the elegant restaurant or the art show) or reflect your personality (maybe you're a dog lover or passionate about the environment). Even though these don't illustrate anything about your acting ability, they tell a story. That story rounds out who you are.

Curating social media to represent not only your brand but also personality is also a great way to start developing and illustrating your versatility. It's a way to say, "You may not see this in me now, but I guarantee you the more you get to know me and the more you work with me, you're going to see I have more facets than what you initially saw." It's not just your castability that gets you the role, it's also your sensibility.

When your brand is clear and developed, you can start to expand it. Developing content for social media is the perfect way to expand the industry's perception of you visually: you in your sweats with your hair looking like you just woke up, versus you polished and ready for a high-power meeting, versus you hanging out at the beach on the weekend with two dogs. They're all different images, but still reflect the many aspects of you.

This is also an opportunity to create visual representations of your "special skills" section on your resumé. If you're fluent in Portuguese, let's see a video or images that celebrate you engaging with that culture, maybe with captions in Portuguese. Are you a registered nurse? Do you play rugby or basketball, or dance? All of these sides of you help fellow creatives understand the type of person you are and the type of roles you can play—and they can all be represented in content on social media.

It's also important to be consistent across all platforms. Yes, each platform serves a slightly different purpose — LinkedIn is very different than Instagram — but your brand, personality, and message can still be the same. You can achieve a consistent tone and feel. And when I say "all platforms," I mean it. Every single place you exist online is discoverable by the industry: charity 5Ks, summer-camp counseling, dating apps. Make sure you're happy with the way you're being represented everywhere.

When I get a submission from an actor, first, I look at their face. If I think that's a cool look for this role, then I turn it over and look at their resumé. If I'm intrigued, the next thing I do is Google them. Think of your digital life as breadcrumbs. Maybe I'll visit your website first, and spend a few minutes there before clicking through to Twitter. That's also linked to your Instagram, where I go next, and so on and so forth. If it's curated wisely, I'll get a positive impression of you in a short amount of time. In other words, don't post every single picture you take and idea you have. (This goes for headshots too. I had an actor send me to her website where she had posted 12 pictures, and five of them were of the same type. Choose one shot per type!)

One last word of caution about social media. Since industry people can and hopefully will scroll your pages, be careful about what you say. I would caution against being snarky or flippantly critical about anyone in the industry or the work they've produced. And when it comes to social justice, while it is incredibly important to stand up for what you believe in, be careful not to jump on bandwagons that haven't been researched. Think before you post.

For this and other reasons, many people like to have both public and private accounts. Your public-facing pages are good informational platforms for people to see your work and get to know you. Direct people in the business toward those. Then, have private accounts where you can be more casual visually and verbally.

Website

To use a digital analogy, think of your website as the splash page for your entire online presence. It's where people will likely go first, and from there, you can launch them off into other platforms you most want them to see.

I'm not going to tell you how to build it — especially when there are plenty of services out there that will do it for you — but I can tell you what to put on it. As we move deeper into the gig economy, creatives pick up more and more hyphens. The actor-writer of 20 years ago is now an actor-writer-director–editor-producer-standup-improviser. The question is what should you highlight on this site? You can't advertise seven different careers on one website! When you try to be too many things or define yourself too broadly, you dilute yourself and the profession you want to be known for. Should I be looking at your website because I want to hire a producer or an actor? Someone coming to your website needs to know who you are and what you want to do. Choose the two — or three, tops — that best represent your skills and goals, and which also make sense with each other. Then, create little breakdown boxes for each on your website, maybe a separate page for each.

That doesn't mean you can't mention your secondary or auxiliary talents. It just means you don't showcase them as much as your top goals. Maybe you include a paragraph somewhere about your other talents and work, with clickthrough links to examples of that work appearing elsewhere. This is especially true for sideline jobs.

Let's say, for example, you're a talented photographer, in addition to being an actor. Certainly mention that somewhere on your website, because if someone is on your actor site, and they see that you're a photographer, they might want to hire you to take their head shots. But you should link them through to a different website that specifically promotes your photography business. "Actor-photographer" is confusing. "Actor who sometimes wears a photographer hat" makes much more sense.

Another note on websites: they can be a great place to house photo galleries that feel too specific or inappropriate for social media. Say you did a Shakespeare Festival in Oregon last summer, and played a 70-year-old. You have these amazing photos from summer stock and want them to live somewhere. But aging up to 70 doesn't translate to TV and film. And Shakespearean stage work doesn't show you in a contemporary light. They're probably not right for Instagram, but they can live in your theatre photo gallery. At the same time, these photos suggest you're a highly trained actor with gravitas and serious chops, who can play different time periods, genres, and ages. Plus, it was at a major festival or national repertory company. A gallery on your website is the perfect place to house these.

Here are the basic pieces of information that must live on your website:

1. Welcome/landing page Use a headshot or a few photos in a triptych that highlight your personality and include your tagline or something appropriate to your brand and type. Use colors, design, and creativity that look professional but still reflect elements of your personality. Include hints of your special skill(s) if applicable. I asked a young actress to move a picture of her puppeteering to her landing page. When she was signed by a manager it was the first thing he mentioned. He said "it made her stand out and it was memorable." Professional information, like a resumé, does not belong on a landing page.

2. Headshot(s) Put at least two or three photos here. These photos should suggest type and castability. There is no need to use multiple photos that basically deliver the same information. I worked with an actress who had a number of modeling photos on her website in the same outfit but different poses over and over. That is a bad use of limited real estate and is ultimately counterproductive. Industry professionals want there to be a concise package of materials that are curated with intention. Five photos of the same look do not communicate that. Usually, I suggest including one comedic or commercial, which might be a smiling shot or something more open and inviting; a dramatic or "edgy" shot, which is good for primetime drama or theatre; and then a charactery or playful photo. The latter can be shot a little differently than a headshot if you want and can be an image from your Instagram that has been effective branding-wise. Final word: You are welcome to show as many looks as you want, if they are each a different variation of your type and brand.

3. Resumé Your resumé should be on one page and should lead with your most professional credits. Your musical theatre resumé could be on one page, and your straight acting resumé could be on another. You can even make a mini-resumé for commercials if you have a number of spots running. How

cool is that? You wouldn't usually pass out three resumés to an agent, but you can show that range of talent and credits on your website. And if you are already working with an agent, they have a choice of which resumé to download and forward on to a casting director. The easier you make their job, the more auditions and jobs you'll get! Update frequently!

4. Bio This should be one to three short paragraphs and include things not found on your resumé. Know that the reader is visiting the page with limited time and attention. I like to call it a "Bio Sandwich."

(a) Start with something personal and inviting: an intro to you, your name, your pronouns, your upbringing, your birth order. Anything that paints an opening picture of you and what informed your career pursuit as an actor.

(b) Put the most relevant credits in the middle. What's been the shining moment thus far? This is a great place to include organizations where you contribute your creative talent (Outreach) as well.

(c) End with three things that exemplify who you are outside of the audition room.

(d) Here is a sample Bio for you to look at:

Taylor Givens (they/them) is a BFA theatre major at _____ University and a Nashville native who embraces their Southern upbringing and has never met a grit they didn't like! The youngest of seven, Taylor needed lots of costumes, a good sense of comedy, and performing to survive the rigors of their academics and their crazy large family!

With interest in classical theatre, specifically Shakespeare, Taylor has been a member of the Tennessee Thespians for the past 10 years and has worked on regional stages in New York, Oregon and California, the latter being at the Old Globe in San Diego, their absolute favorite. The goal of sharing Shakespeare with young artists is a mission Taylor will pay forward through the non-profit online program they created for actors 8-16 years old, called Tater Tot Thespians, aka TTT. When not buried in Iambic pentameter, Taylor is an accomplished Step dancer, frisbee lover (especially with their dog, Woofee) and the current national pogo stick champion .

Bottom line: You can talk about your interests, your personal views, and show a sense of humor. The more agents and casting directors know you, like you, and trust you, the more people will hire you.

5. Sizzle reels A sizzle reel is a short, fun, fast-paced "trailer" of your clips from TV series and films and will be the first thing an agent or casting director will look at. It should be 1 to 1.5 minutes long, easy to watch, and show your range. Avoid using a clip where you have just a reaction, like a scream or laughing attack. Those do not help us see you connecting and relating in a scene. Also, please keep this reel to work that is current and relevant to who you are now. If you have a great credit from five years ago, then let that live as a separate clip on the website. It's important that this sizzle is as close to your age and look as possible.

6. Photo gallery Twitter, Instagram, and Facebook, give us information about you personally as well as professionally. The more events you attend, and sports, charities, play readings, and workshops you're involved in, the more photos you can post. Use the real estate on your website to call attention to these facets of your life. Think about what can enhance your marketability as an actor. Show that you're not only proactive with your acting career but you have a fascinating and robust life outside of it as well.

7. Contact page Until my last project, I would have said to just list your Instagram and email for contacting. However, the last time I was searching for someone specific for a project, this person had no representation, but was on Instagram and had a contact form through her website. I DM'd her first and didn't get an answer so I filled out her contact form. That's when I heard from her! Contact pages are also a great way to keep a safe distance during initial messaging. Use a business email (or Google Voice) and vet who is reaching out to you before giving them personal contact information in reply. I have seen fun ways to label this in the section headers of a website. Instead of "contact" think of ways to compel them to use the form! Maybe "Call Me?" That is an eyecatcher since no-one is invited to call anymore!

Promote your brand and platform

You've determined your brand. You developed a bunch of content to illustrate it. And you built the social-media "galleries" in which to continue showcasing content that represents you. Now, with a little savvy, the squeaky wheel will get the grease! In other words, work it! It won't take you long to read or understand directives for various projects, but it may take time to perfect the execution of them.

Social media

Maintain your social media.

- Set a posting schedule. Maybe you post once a day or once every other day.
- Develop campaigns. If you're a free-spirited hippie chick, maybe you do #fridayflowers; if you're an inspirational kind of person, #motivationmondays.

Build relationships with your audience.

- Respond to comments. Ask questions in posts ("What flower should I post tomorrow?").
- Actively seek the audience who will connect with you by following them or commenting on their posts, or by commenting on the posts of people whose brands are similar to yours, in order to reach their audiences.

I'm not going to tell you how to become an influencer or advise on the use of hashtags or analytics. That's not the point. The point is to keep putting out the best version of yourself—the one you want the industry to see. Until you have a lot of credits, your website and social media platforms are where the industry will look, and I guarantee they will look.

Acting reels

Avoid the generic reel. Posting a "Drama reel" or "Comedic reel" is like asking a casting professional to guess "what's behind door 1 or door 2." As a busy casting director, I don't have time to watch reels if there's no guarantee that what's in there will be relevant to my search. Help people find what they're looking for and compel them to watch by posting specific clips with titles that are interesting and also give a little more information. Maybe you post a clip titled "Awkward camp moment" or "Dating in your 30s." Then the casting director might think, "that's what I'm looking for," or, at least, "that could be fun to watch." This kind of marketing strategy, combined with your specific look, might be the exact combination needed for the role.

Capitalizing on work

Every job you get, you bring your Head of Marketing along. You can't just think that any job will naturally lead to more. Rather, your Head of Marketing will take specific actions to make sure you get more work. When you are starting out, you may not command a high salary but you can still be compensated in other ways. Maybe as part of the deal you can get the clip of your scene from the project. Follow up with producers: When will I get my footage of the film? Does the film have a release date? Can I put my footage on my website? Can I put a blast on my Instagram? Can I take a picture of me on set in costume and post it? What can I do to capitalize on this opportunity now and market and brand it?

This department has to follow you as you go forward and look for opportunities to let the world know, "Hey, this is what I'm doing / where I just was / the job I just booked." Let's say an agent just heard about you through somebody on set, and they're like, "We heard you did a really good job on set. We'd like to meet you. Do you have any of the footage from what you did?" Imagine being able to respond, "As a matter of fact, I do have my footage and I'll send it to you and thank you so much for reaching out to me."

Closing thoughts

Your brand is not every facet of you. It's probably the most marketable one and the best way to launch your career. There is a way to be both artistically authentic and industry savvy. Your Head of Marketing will help you do that. Meanwhile, your Head of Biz Development will be working to grow that nuanced, varied, artistically fulfilling future career. Let's meet them now.

6

Head of Business Development (Biz Dev)

A typical day for your Head of Biz Dev might start with reading all of the industry "trades," then emailing a producer you met at a party to congratulate them on a pilot order that was just written up in *Variety*, and then opening up your database of contacts to add entries for everyone you met at last night's screening of a friend's short film. Just like breakfast or physical activity, this should be a part of every day.

These Head of Biz Dev duties needn't take much time, but they must be done regularly:

- **Stay informed.** Read all trades, publications, listen to podcasts, and soak up relevant information in your industry.
- **Build a contact database.** Keep your contacts organized and maintain detailed histories for each.
- **Maintain correspondence.** Follow up with new connections. Circle back to past connections. Identify and pursue like-minded creatives.
- **Publicize yourself.** Put on your sales hat and toot your own horn.
- **Work toward getting representation.** Make sure you're ready first.

Stay informed

This part is simple: learn about the industry every day. Listen to podcasts, read industry related news, keep yourself current on the business you are entering. You want to know not only what specific projects are selling and being produced, but also what kind of shows and films each network and production company makes, the tone of their slate, the genres they make. Stay informed of who has first look deals with companies you are interested in working with.

Each platform is promoting itself, too. The kinds of shows they produce comprise the brand of the platform and its distinct way of speaking to its audience. They are telling you, "if you watch our content, this is what you'll get." With a greater understanding of their taste and business model, you'll be able to submit yourself for specific roles (next chapter) existing under the umbrellas of those networks or production companies.

Stay ahead of opportunity, a case study

If opportunity knocks in this business, it may or may not be through an agent or manager. Most likely it will come from your own tenacity to look for work and the intentional inroads made towards the projects you are interested in.

Artists who have cultivated relationships and kept on top of where fellow creatives are and what they are doing, are the ones who advance their careers. This requires staying informed.

In the industry, projects that are going into the pipeline are announced all the time in publications like *Variety*, *Deadline*, *The Hollywood Reporter*, and *Backstage*. There are also great podcasts like HR's "TV's Top Five," "The Business with Kim Masters," and other resources.

I know a young actress who is a shining example of this. She listens and reads all the time. She makes notes when she sees a favorite book or news story in development. She scans the producers, directors, and casting teams assigned to these projects and she puts on her Biz Dev hat!

One example of this is when she saw a post in *Deadline* and took note of the creatives involved. The project had a "first-look" deal with a streamer that from the description, not only fit the kind of projects that really spoke to her as a creative, but also as a human being. She proceeded to research the producer of the project on social media, trying to find more information and found that a mutual friend followed this producer!

She then reached out to this friend and through a series of connections she took the reins and asked if her resumé and film clip could be sent on her behalf. Shortly thereafter, the producer got back to this mutual friend and was complimentary of the tenacity and initiative this actress had displayed. Now the next step will be to follow this project and reach out directly when the time is right.

You never know who will take a chance, watch your materials, or answer an email. When you do make connections, use IMDb to follow those creatives. You can join IMDb for free. It's a service that provides a searchable database "of more than 1.8 million movies, TV and entertainment programs and more than 3.8 million cast and crew members." IMDbPro is a subscription service designed for professionals who work in the industry and is much more comprehensive with valuable contact information. It's purchased through Amazon.

Build a contact database

You must take the time to do this. You can't just think you're going to remember that "you had coffee with someone a few years ago, and it was an introduction made by your friend Greg" and then start searching through your Gmail to find it. Don't create future problems for yourself.

Update your database weekly. Create an organized system with multiple ways to reference it. As your career grows, and you make more and more connections, it will be increasingly important to have them organized so you can quickly find people.

I suggest having separate databases for personal contacts and professional contacts. The people in your professional life are not just casting directors, agents, and managers, who help you get hired. It's also all of the people you interface with while doing creative jobs in the industry: writers, ADs, PAs, makeup artists, etc. Your personal database are the people you've established real relationships with, people you wouldn't hesitate to ask a favor of, confide in, or reciprocate the same. These people are your posse, your fellow creatives and close friends. For every entry, include what they do, where and how you met, who you know in common, when and why you've reached out before, and any important interests you share. Several services are available to help you keep everything organized. For example, both iCloud and Google Contacts allow you to create lists and add relevant people. Another great resource is IMDbPro, where you can use their "Pages You Track" feature. This feature allows you to catalog both professionals you currently work with or aspire to work with in the future.

The last piece of this database should center around locale and where you choose to live. Consider where your strongest connections are to start out. If you're looking to move to another city/marketplace, take a good look at the contacts you have in that locale before making a professional decision to move.

When opportunity knocks, a case study

Once, after I spoke to a group of performers at SAG/AFTRA, an attendee stood during the open discussion afterwards to pose a question. "I am an actress and want to pursue that as my main focus," she said. "I've been approached to help produce a small independent film, out of town. I'm conflicted about whether or not I should do this. If I leave I am not available to go on auditions. Do you think I should do this?"

I patiently waited while she spoke a little longer about the people involved, the job she would have and the contacts she would make (all the while, answering her own question). Needless to say, I told her she should 100% take this opportunity. Here are my reasons:

1 There is nothing active in waiting. She can still tape auditions, follow opportunities, and stay involved from afar, while meeting, working, and interfacing with other creatives.

2 All the people on a set—PAs, set design, props, DP's, makeup, wardrobe, lighting, etc.—are ALL fellow creatives, working to move up and get better at their craft. Why not work with them, make them part of your Biz Dev department, and create more community?

3 This opportunity will give her more experience in another facet of the business. She will learn from this situation and grow as a working professional. Afterward, she will have a new confidence as an actress. The knowledge and experience will follow her into the room.

To be clear, I'm not suggesting you get distracted by an opportunity that is counterintuitive to your objectives. But, if you find an opportunity that's "career adjacent" it can be a wonderful way to move forward.

Maintain correspondence

If you make a real connection with, or have an opportunity to stay connected with someone in the industry—maybe an agent, manager, casting director, director, or any fellow creative in the business—the most important thing is to maintain correspondence with that person over time. Even if you don't have anything to share about yourself or your work, you should still reach out. The point is to give before you ask. Understand that our business is based on relationships. Real relationships. Put your efforts into establishing yourself as a supporter and an ally first. See the person as the accomplished professional that they are and celebrate that. Perhaps you are reading the news and see that a director you recently met scored work on an exciting project. You should absolutely reach out to congratulate them. It's such an easy way to stay in touch by giving instead of asking.

Another reason to reach out is if you see an announcement about a project in pre production. Maybe you know someone who is "above the line" (meaning they're involved in the creative process, as opposed to "below the line," which is cast and crew involved in the actual production). If you do know or have a connection to a director, producer, screenwriter, or casting director, absolutely reach out. Students ask me all the time: "If a writer or director asks for me, does that mean I'll get an audition?" Absolutely.

Another opportunity for correspondence would be if you're involved with some charity work you're excited about or proud of, and you invite a couple of contacts to be your guests at an upcoming fundraiser event. You don't want to email someone the day after you met them and ask for help with your career.

Anyone you meet that you felt a genuine connection with, follow up with them through correspondence! Be fearless—just don't be greedy. Email the person to say thanks and it was nice to meet them and refer to something that was a shared moment in your conversation. If they ask you to forward your materials, then and only then, share one of your clips and thank them for being a supporter of the arts. One other opportunity is to just send the follow-up email and include all of your links at the bottom of your email signature. If they want to click, they will.

People mean what they say, a case study

I find actors to be very resourceful when it comes to finding and making connections. What they seem inherently unable to do is follow up on them. I had a student tell me once that a casting director approached her after a solo show, told her how much she enjoyed the performance, and gave her a business card. I said, "That's great! What happened?"

And she said, "Nothing. I haven't reached out to her." I would say I was astonished, but I've seen this happen too many times. My student said she didn't want to bother this woman, who is surely very busy. She thought maybe the casting director was "just being nice" and didn't actually want to hear from her. And on and on.

"She could have just left!" I said. "Why would she take the time to approach you after the show, if she didn't want to hear from you? Why would she literally give you her contact information if she didn't want to hear from you?"

I'm mentioning this anecdote now because it illustrates a specific kind of reluctance and shyness that I see overwhelming my students over and over again.

I certainly understand why actors are sometimes reluctant to do this. In the entertainment industry, the line between colleagues and friends is blurred. This business is built on relationships, not transactions. It's hard to know where you stand and you never want to come on too strong. But if you're always giving first and asking later, you'll never go wrong. Build your network first: look for connections and ways to support other people. Only afterward should you approach with an ask.

Ok, so what about when you do have something to share in your career, or you are in a position where you feel ready to ask a favor? I have a basic template I suggest for this kind of industry correspondence.

WORKSHEET 8: Letter Writing Template

Give, Want, Why, and Personalization. It's pretty simple and intuitive, but my students have found it helpful over the years.

The Give is the introduction, wherein you explain why you're reaching out to this person specifically. "I'm writing to tell you how inspired I am by your contribution to women in film. . ." "I'm writing to tell you that your influence has propelled me to get involved in. . ." "I heard you're involved in [such and such] project. Congratulations! I continue to be inspired by your success."

The Want is the request. What are you hoping they will do or help you with? Maybe you are hoping to come in for a meeting. Or you're in a play and want them to come see it. Maybe you're hoping for an introduction by them to someone else. Don't be coy. Be clear.

The Why is when you demonstrate your worthiness to receive this attention or help. Why are you a good candidate for a meeting? Why is this play and your work in it worth their time?

The Personalization is your chance to endear yourself with this person and remind them of whatever connection you share that goes beyond work. If at some point you discovered you share a love of knitting, you could ask how that quilt is coming along. Or maybe you both have huskies and you want to check in on their dog. You get the idea.

I often help my students with their letters. See the below example of a student's first draft, my notes on it, and then the second draft.

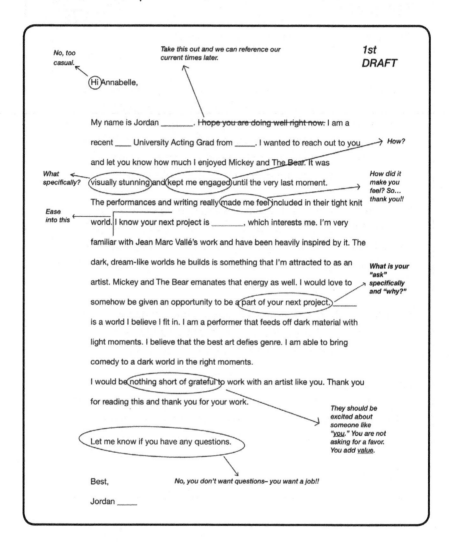

Here is the letter with my suggested changes:

Dear Annabelle,

Hi! My name is Jordan _____ and I'm a recent _____ University Acting graduate from _____. Needless to say, this is a unprecedented time to be entering into the industry and when a filmmaker creates art that inspires me, I'm compelled to reach out.

Mickey and The Bear resonated with me in many ways, especially the themes of unrealized potential and the breaking free from complacency. Mickey's struggle and eventual break for freedom exemplified resilience which I really appreciate in the world right now. So I want to thank you for a film that will stay with me for quite some time to come.

Upon reading that your next project will be _____, I felt compelled to contact you. I'm very familiar with Jean-Marc Vallé's work and your collaboration with him is a dream project. The opportunity to be on set, as either cast or crew, would be an extremely valuable experience. It is a career goal of mine to work with artists like you.

I'm ready to break out and take the world by storm!

Best,

Jordan _____

It's so important to maintain authentic relationships. Likely, you'll become friends with some of these people—not because you're hoping to get something out of it, but because you genuinely like each other. You follow each other on Instagram, and are learning and sharing more about your lives. Eventually, those emails may turn into coffee dates. If so, never assume it's a business meeting unless that's explicitly been discussed in advance.

Industry relationships can be tricky, especially for those in the relationship who are up-and-coming. But if you keep your relationships focused on the other person, and take time and care to circle back and stay supportive, there will be dividends on the other side.

Publicize yourself

Until you can afford to pay a publicist, you are responsible for all of that work. You must let people know what you're up to. It's your job to create awareness around who you are and what you're doing. It's your job to figure out ways to create buzz around you and your projects.

Obviously, this kind of correspondence is more pointed and salesy by nature. You do it the exact same way a professional does: single out the things that are interesting about you and your projects, and communicate the most important points people should know. Figure out what the hook is.

Much publicity happens on social media these days. Instagram and Twitter campaigns can be especially effective at connecting with fans because the platforms are dynamic and fun. If you get booked in a vampire show, start hash tagging and posting about vampire content right away. By the time your show premieres, you will have found that community and can access it with the news you want to share.

Don't give up on old-school methods. Build an email list. Start now. It's a numbers game, so the more you have, the higher your rate of return. Also, lean into groups: do you have an alumni organization in your city? Are you active in a church group? Reaching out to your non-industry communities is especially effective, as these people are not getting 100 emails or invites a day and it creates a fan base of supporters that are invested and find value in entertainment.

Work towards getting representation

It may take some time before you are represented properly by an agent or manager. Until then, you'll have to represent yourself. (I've dedicated the following chapter to explaining how.) At the same time, you should always be working toward representation. The number-one question my students ask me is, "How do I get an agent?" The number two question: "Can you help me get an agent?"

The issue is, if you barely have any credits, how do you begin? You need certain tools in place in order to be a candidate worthy of representation. Without some kind of content that you've developed for yourself, how can a rep make a decision about whether or not you are ready to be represented, and whether or not you would fit in with their roster and aesthetic? If you haven't been in anything professional, then it's on you to go out and create content so people will have a way to understand what you do. Liaise with your Head of Marketing to make sure you have the materials in place that will allow someone to take a good look at you and get an overall feeling of what you do and how you do it. Some agencies are known for talent development. Others only take on talent once smaller agents have developed them. Be savvy and only target those agencies who work with emerging artists.

Then, you'll likely have to rely on word-of-mouth and your own networking system. Very few people are discovered from general submissions. Instead, ask fellow creatives for advice and, if it's a good fit, referrals. If you are still in an undergrad BFA program, you should become hyper focused on the single most important objective you feel you need as you are starting to prepare for the industry. Seek out advice to the fullest extent it is available to you. Understand that ultimately, these programs are there to train you, but not necessarily to transition you. So, if you don't get satisfactory answers from within your program, the reality is you will have to take these focused objectives into your own hands and find other sources of information and mentorship. Attend industry nights. Try to get booked in showcase events. Research the list of accredited talent agencies and target the smaller, boutique firms and management companies that have attended showcases and panels in the past. Ask fellow creatives and teachers connected to the industry for advice and introductions as well.

Closing thoughts

I know, I know: there is so much work before there is actual work. But the fulsome career you want to have needs a strong foundation beneath it. Because of all this work you've put in, you now know everything there is to know about the jobs you're right for and the jobs you want; you have relationships with people in a wide variety of capacities all over the industry, and you are practiced at getting the word out about who you are and what you do. Skill sets: check, check, and check. Plus, of course, you are educated, talented, and skilled in the craft itself.

You are ready to go get those jobs. Let's see how your Head of Representation will make it happen.

7

Head of Representation

Representing yourself: It's an uncomfortable idea to swallow. I can tell you that until you have an agent or manager, you have no other choice but to represent yourself. That's just the truth. But I also recognize that this truism isn't very encouraging.

Here's a more motivating way to frame it: When it is time to get an agent and manager, they will only want to work with you if you already know who you are and how to represent yourself. Knowing how to rep yourself suggests that you are resourceful, capable, and savvy. If there is nothing else I teach you in this book, it will be the value of being industrious.

I know submitting yourself is scary. I get it. But it will get easier each time. Take your feelings out of it. Remember that these gatekeepers are not there to keep you out. Rather, they need you. They are looking for talent to hire. They want to hear from you. You've got to re-orient the way you understand the process of submitting yourself. Now is the time to put yourself out there. Here's how to do it.

The Head of Representation has six main job duties.

- **Find places to submit yourself.** Know where to look and how to identify which opportunities are worth your time.
- **Efficiently read breakdowns.** Determine whether you are right for a role based on certain specific breakdown components.
- **Master the technical aspects of the self-tape.** Follow this checklist in order to look professional and present your best self.
- **Make strong choices for the self-tape.** Learn how to trust your instincts in the virtual audition world.
- **Shine in the meetings you get.** Do your research in advance, stay present, follow up, and have content ready to go.
- **Revisit headshots.** From time to time, you will need to re-shoot.

Find places to submit yourself

Determine whether or not it is worth your time to submit. Not every breakdown holds the key to the right job. When you look at job postings, ask yourself how that type is represented in the real world.

I have compiled a few resources my students and I have collected over the years. Start with these suggestions and add to them to make your own list. Some of these are subscription services, so make sure they serve you in the best way possible and be discerning. Remember, if there is a cost involved, make sure your CFO has it in the budget. Another way to sample these services is to take advantage of free profiles and free one-month trials (but remember to cancel them!). The leading ones are Actors Access, Backstage, Casting Networks, Casting Frontier, and Cast It Talent. For more ideas, visit the link below.

 https://bloomsbury.pub/acting-business

Know your specific type, a case study

I had an actress recently who said, "I submitted myself for a conservative news anchor." And I said, "Is it a field representative or is it the anchor who sits with the two other co-hosts?" Anchors are very shiny and polished. There's a very specific look to those news anchors. Field reporters are a little more diverse in look and body type, right?

And what network? FOX? MSNBC? CNN? This actress can certainly play "professional"—but "conservative" feels like a buzz word to me. That's a type we can look at in media and recognize. This actress is not that type and does not have that sensibility. Could she play one? Sure. Is it worth her time to submit for a job when she doesn't have the essence of the part, and there are so many other jobs she can spend her time submitting for? Probably not. It's not always best to throw "spaghetti at the wall" and see what sticks. That can sometimes signal a lack of awareness. Even agents can be guilty of that. I released a breakdown once and the same actress was submitted for every single role on it. That's really not a good tactic.

Now, to understand whether you are better suited as, for example, an anchor or a field reporter, you'll need to know how to read a breakdown.

Efficiently read breakdowns

Sticking with our network-news-anchor role, let's say you do have that look, and you want to submit. What can you learn from the breakdown that will help you prepare for your self tape? Consider the context around the role.

Other than what we've already discussed, ask other questions. Who's producing the show? Does your Head of Business Development already have a good feeling for the kinds of shows and characters this company or studio creates? If not, research. Also, on what platform or network will this live? Again, your Head of Biz Dev should already be familiar with the existing shows and target markets of each platform and network, which tells you even more about what this character will look like and how they will behave.

Can you get a feeling for the tone of the show? Is it bright or dark, poppy or moody, etc.? Is there any information about the social/economical/geographical demographics of the character or the world? Don't just read the phrase "sassy and ambitious newsperson" and think you know who that is.

A great example on how to evaluate locale and genre would be to consider *Bloodline, Succession,* and *Yellowstone.* They are similar shows: patriarchal father, enabling mother, brothers and a sister navigating power dynamics, and everyone keeping secrets. It's very King Lear. But these very similar-seeming shows are placed in completely different geographical locations (Florida Keys, Manhattan, and Montana), and therefore everything about these shows are different. The characters who belong in one world do not belong in the other. They dress differently. They carry themselves differently. They speak differently. The fabric of their worlds is different.

Geography and local culture determine much about a character—and little of that will appear in a breakdown. Sometimes, you have to read between the lines.

I also want to take a moment to discuss compromises, specifically the compromises you are and are not willing to make depending on professional demands. Are there some things you will never ever do or, some things you normally wouldn't do, but might, depending on the director or how good the clip could be for your career? With streaming, shows are grittier, more graphic and violent. It's important to understand the world the producers and writers are creating. Look closely for story line and the character you would be playing. I spoke about this earlier, in the HR chapter. It's worth mentioning again here, because when the breakdown is released, you may be faced with some tough decisions.

You can prepare by asking yourself (and your agent, if you have one) hard questions now and paying attention to the breakdown specifications.

Master the technical aspects of the self-tape

Everything I'm about to tell you seems self-explanatory, but you'd be surprised by the poor quality of so many tapes I see. Below are your basic criteria and how to meet them. First, a general tip: If you can, designate a space in your home as your self-tape studio. Choose a place that's mostly soundproof. You'll only have to set up several of the criteria below once.

Lighting

Invest in some form of good lighting. I love a standing ring light because they are easy to use. Your camera or smartphone can be placed in the center. You can also get a tiny ring light that clips onto your smartphone or a moveable ring light on a tripod.

Don't spend a crazy amount of money on lighting. You can use existing overhead lighting, lamps, or natural light to your benefit by understanding the principles of three- and four-point lighting. Basically, you want a principal light to be pointing right at you, probably a little bit to the side. Its purpose is to light you. Then, you want a second light to be filling out the space, lighting up the background, and removing some of the shadow. Finally, you want a backlight to sculpt and separate you from your background. No matter the number of light sources you use, make sure you're covering those three bases. YouTube tutorials can help you out a lot here.

Sound

Usually, the microphone on your camera or smartphone is good enough, but if you're hearing fuzz or buzzing, there are programs like Audacity, Kapwing, AudioRemover, and iMovie that will reduce unwanted noise in your tape.

Also—again, it seems obvious but you'd be surprised—if a trash truck passes your apartment in the middle of a take, if your fish tank is gurgling, if your dog is barking, if your cat is scratching at the door... basically any unwanted distractions, you need to stop and start over.

Background

Declutter your background. As a casting director, I'm supposed to be looking at you. If you stand in the doorway, and there's a light switch to your left and a picture hanging on the wall to your right, and there's something stuck to the corner of the door, all of that clutter distracts me. Don't give me a reason to be distracted. If you have the money, you can buy one of those pop up backgrounds that opens into a large piece of fabric on a wire frame. Or, hang a bed sheet, curtain, or even a yoga mat. Keep it simple and clean. If you decide to use a "set" like background, keep reading. I've addressed that under "Make strong choices for the Self Tape."

Readers

It's best to have a skilled reader to help make the acting come alive. Try to make sure the voice on the other end of the tape is someone who will help your audition and enhance your performance. Preferably, find another actor who will give you something to work with. With the new paradigm of Zoom self-tapes and auditions, it is important to make sure that the audio of your reader is clear and that it is not just in voice, but in visual, that way you have someone to connect with. Create as much of a live connection as possible, and realize that self-tapes are often not just about the words you say, but about your ability to connect and listen to someone else. On a recent project, I had an actor submit his tape only doing the lines assigned for his character. No other actor. No other reactions to somebody speaking to him, and he wrote a note to me saying it didn't really matter since he was taking license to create the character and the focus was on him anyway. It's the first time that I actually wrote a note back and told him "I'm sorry, but it's not just about you." I'm interested in the quiet moments, the struggle with information that's coming to you and how you process it, as much or more than the actual words you say.

Editing and uploading

Casting directors are short on time. Don't send a file with extra content or empty space at the start. Cut it down if it needs to be edited.

Upload it through a platform that will make it very easy for us to watch. Don't make someone go through too many steps just to watch you. Choose a platform that will condense your video so it won't take forever to upload or download. Trial and error is your friend here.

Send your self-tape to a friend first as a test. Know what works for you before the morning your tape is due.

When you send your tape, and it is through a platform that needs a password, pick something that is simple and intuitive to the project and not personal. In other words, if the project name is "The Best Ever," put either the character name or project title as the password. Once I have access to the content, be sure to thoroughly label who you are, the role, and the project name. Label your content appropriately from the very first iteration all the way through to the end of the process. If things are not properly labeled, they will be thrown away or unwatched.

Your file size for Actors Access should be 640×480 and anything larger, i.e. 720, will be downsized by the system and you may notice the quality being compromised when you revert to full screen. The reason is most casting directors will watch video for information on a small screen and not blow it up to full screen. Since this conversation of file size is one that is currently under review, it is best to contact Breakdown Services to find out about the most updated delivery system information.

A final note on submissions: please don't send materials that are a series of reactions edited together or a one line role from a movie that serves the locale or storyline and has no real character development. Send us something where you are front and center and the focus is on you. I see actors make this mistake a lot.

Make strong choices for the self-tape

The atmosphere in the audition room has changed significantly. Pre-pandemic, there was a healthy combination of in-person pre-reads and callback auditions. The chance to meet in person and gain insight from the casting director about the script and direction of the project with the chance to be re-directed was a welcome part of the process for both the actor and the casting director. This balance was challenged by the pandemic. It created a need to pivot and maintain a pipeline to see talent. Actors who might have submitted a self-tape in the early stages of auditioning are now finding that the entire process has gone online. Being asked to re-submit and take direction, and even chemistry reads, are now happening in Zoom or Eco Cast sessions. So, how does an actor make choices in a vacuum? How can the work that you do on a role and the energy you put into the audition translate into a computer screen? How do you work the room? How do you feel the energy that is (or isn't) coming toward you? How much of it matters in the long run?

The steps to creating a successful self-tape for a role are actually more in your control than you think. Here are some steps that can create a memorable audition and help the casting director see you in the role.

1 Create a small amount of production value. Whereas before in the room there were imperatives to not invade the space of the casting director, keep focused on the reader in the room and not use the room as a set, those elements can change for a self-tape. If you are filming a role with a workplace setting, you can set up your camera in your home office and use the background to create a sense of place. It's true that most casting directors would prefer a simple, standard background that's free of distraction and uniform in color. The purpose of the self-tape is to watch your performance. However, if you are not able to access a clean space to tape in, integrate what you do have access to and make it work for the scene. These "sets" must be simple, and not distracting. You can pick up a prop if you would like to use one, you can talk from behind a desk, you can enter a room. In other words, you can give us a sense of the scene through your surroundings. You may choose to do something like this even if you do have a simple, standard background. As long as added production values are subtle and make sense for the scene, they might help you clinch the deal. For example, Stephanie Hsu's audition for *Everything Everywhere All at Once* broke the mold in a few revelatory ways, which actors are taking inspiration from after it was posted online. Long story short: don't be afraid to create a sense of place or a bit of drama, just not at the expense of your own performance.

2 Spend a few minutes in your slate to say hello and let us meet you as a person and not as the "actor wanting the job." Yes, we need the slate to contain your vital information (name, location, and if asked, physical stats) but you should also use the opportunity to be personable in your slate. If you know who you are auditioning for you can say hello to them by name and you can thank and acknowledge the opportunity to audition.

3 As discussed, have a good reader whenever possible. It's about the give and take between two people. It's about listening, as much if not more, than speaking. As stated above, if there isn't a person there to help, they can be on Zoom, but make sure you can connect and react to someone. It is impossible to act and collaborate as a party of one.

4 Do multiple takes. This is probably the best part of virtual auditioning. Sometimes we are incredibly prepared and then there are a series of

factors that waylay us or diminish our performance. Long waits at auditions when the session is running behind, nerves once we get in the room or stresses from the trip to the audition like trouble parking, a late train or an unexpected expense for an Uber or taxi when the train didn't come at all! None of that is an issue with the chance to self-tape and choose your best take to upload. All the creative control is yours. You can try multiple approaches and decide which one represents your work in the best light. The other advantage is the filming can be done to fit your work schedule and other obligations. You can plan for it, carve out the time and not have to worry about juggling your shift at the restaurant or asking someone to cover for you while you run out and stress about getting back on time. You can create a sense of calm.

5 Do a trial run before you submit your materials. Send them to yourself or a friend to ensure the delivery is foolproof and is watchable, clear, and accessible. Label all your materials with your name and scene. Make sure the audio is clear, the lighting looks good. Sometimes we see something clearly but the delivery mode can corrupt or compromise the content. Troubleshooting will prevent that from happening.

6 Write a note in the Eco-cast section. This is an opportunity to communicate directly with the casting director. For example, if there are dates you will be unavailable during the shoot, rather than simply not submitting, you can take a minute to let them know and respectfully decline the audition and thank them for their interest. Conversely, if there's a note that can enhance the audition, include it. For instance, if we are looking for someone with a special skill inherent to the character, you might want to include a short video marketing that skill. We recently cast a project that required strong stunt and dancing skills. The actor who was cast has a background working at Cirque du Soleil and he included a small sample of him dancing with emphasis on stunt type movements. It got him the role. Overall, this new paradigm for auditioning is kinder to an actor and their schedule. It allows casting to see many more choices for a role, including non-represented actors, and it opens the opportunity to create more content that you can use for marketing yourself. Embrace this opportunity to play with your choices and make a strong impression. Another thing to think about ... we may also share content with our colleagues so be cognizant that this tape may be watched by more than just the casting team for that

specific project. When we have a great tape to work with, we are excited to share your talent. So, get to it!

7 Now that all these technical aspects are taken care of, make sure that whatever you've shot will actually help you get a role or representation. (We'll cover this in depth in the Head of Creative Development chapter, but it's important to mention here as well.) Make sure any piece of content you create shows the types of characters you can play or puts you in situations and roles where you can really shine. Be cognizant of the material you are choosing or have been given, and make impactful choices.

Shine in the meetings you get

Usually, when you're called in to pitch yourself or to have a general meeting, there is no format or expectation. They may just want to meet you because someone mentioned you to them and said you were interesting. They may not have a project in mind for you yet, but just want to know who you are. When an actor walks into my office, I want to learn the most I can about them as a person and what makes them who they are. I can read a resumé and look at films, but when I sit opposite you, I'm looking to make a connection and build a relationship. Until that is established, don't expect professionals to help you.

The main purpose of these kinds of meetings is to find out what you have in common, who you are as people, and how you connect over common issues. You may spend the entirety of the meeting talking about the fact that you both volunteer with shelter dogs. That's a successful meeting!

Still, you should be prepared to take the opportunity to express whatever you most want them to know about you and your work. I use the term "30-second pitch," although you never want it to feel that formal or scripted. Think about it as telling your story in 30 seconds or less. The words you say are only a small part of it! Remember the science of first impressions? We form opinions about people in less than a 10th of a second. In that amount of time, we decide whether someone is trustworthy, competent, extroverted, dominant, and so on. Think about how you telegraph to people who you are, and how you can "have them at hello."

To further articulate this idea, I've broken down the meeting advice into three sections: before, during, and after.

Before the meeting

1 Find out about the person you are meeting with. Where did they work before? What is their background? Where are they from? Do they have a team that they work with? If yes, who else is on the team? Do your homework on the agency, the type of clients they have and other creatives they rep (ie., writers, directors). This is a great talking point to appreciate the other talent they are repping and helping.

2 When you write to set up a meeting, thank them for reaching out and give them a window of time that will work with your schedule. For example: I am in finals and have graduation between now and _____. Any time after _____I am able to meet. OR, I am available to meet anytime between 12–4, M–Thursday. In other words, be specific. Don't write "please let me know what works for you." Give them workable times that you can definitely make and then "look forward to a time that works for them." Keep it simple. Conversely, if they ask for a specific time, unless it's absolutely impossible, say "yes" and show up.

3 Please don't make the emails lengthy or ask a lot of questions before the meeting. They saw your work, briefly corresponded, and now they are asking to learn more about you. It's all good.

4 If the assistant is "cc'd" on the email, direct parking and logistic questions to the assistants. Make sure you get their full name. Put in Biz Dev contacts.

5 Subject line: any of these are fine:
   Hi _____, it's _____(your first and last name.
   Hi _____, met you at the name of school date showcase.
   Reaching out as requested . . .
   Hi_____, responding to your request.
   Looking forward to meeting.
   Thank you for reaching out.
   Thank you for your inquiry!
   Materials you requested (if they asked for pic/resumé and more film).

At the meeting

Apply a "first date" mentality. This is to get to know each other and hopefully step one in **establishing a relationship**. Don't come to the meeting with an "agenda" that inhibits a good flow of conversation. Establish a rapport. It's not a time to bring a list of questions. It's a time to learn more about them, the way they work, and what you have in common.

1 Coming in knowing something about the person and agency is a must. Let that unfold naturally. **It's flattering for them to know you cared enough to learn about them and their journey**. It's also refreshing to meet someone who is interested in conversation and creating a relationship. Don't regale them with shows you've been in, or "inside" moments from school. Use this time as a point of departure into the professional world.

2 **Asking questions is fine. But only as it relates to this situation.** What drew them to your work? If you see yourself working in a particular pocket. . .do they see that, too? Is there a client of theirs with a career that's really inspiring to you? If yes, share that with them. If they signed any other graduates in the past, maybe you can bond over that as well.

3 Having a POV about your acting is fine but acknowledge there is more development happening once you graduate and talk about the projects you are currently planning to develop, shoot, write, and collaborate on while auditioning.

4 **Have fun in these meetings. These are just people who are looking to see if this will be a good relationship and time investment.**

5 **Mention any mentorship in the industry that you have had.** They may/may not know them but will appreciate you mentioning those who have helped you. It's nice to see young artists who are grateful for those who have invested in them and don't act like "they did it alone."

After the meeting

1 DO NOT ASK THEM WHAT'S NEXT. If they ask you, say you are taking a few other meetings but that "this one was your first priority." Keep your confidence up and leave them feeling like the meeting was worthwhile.

2 Thank the assistant on the way out and be sure to send them a thank you.

3 Write a follow up email/note a day later. Refer to some of the things that resonated in the meeting and let them know again how much you would value a working relationship with them. Send them additional materials if you have something else to add to the conversation or if they have asked you for more content.

4 Don't shoot for a long meeting. Let the conversation take its course and then allow them to get back to their busy day. Acknowledge how nice it is to meet in person again. If on Zoom, there are many fun ways to close, I am generally a bit irreverent so my play book is a little different than yours but I always try to use what was talked about, the location they are in, background they chose, or something in common to close with. Let them feel like they were a great part of your day. (Again, it's a win to have these conversations.)

The Bates Executive Presence model

When preparing for meetings, I tell my students to reference the Bates Executive Presence model. It's intended for executives, but it totally works for actors—which you know I think is kismet, considering the concept of this book! The Bates model is all about how you engage with others, align your objectives with theirs, inspire them, and move people to act. It offers a really interesting model when thinking about how to package yourself and tell your story. I won't reprint what you can find online, but can quickly summarize.

What resonates for me in the Bates model are three specific categories: character, substance, and style. Subsets of those categories are authenticity, concern, resonance, and intentionality. Be real. Tap in to the details that are unique to you. Be a good listener. Let incoming information resonate with you and then react to it. Communicate without an agenda. Be vulnerable. It's always better to take a risk than not to share who you are. Let people understand you. Be intentional about who you are and how you communicate. Only when you have an impact on someone can you elicit a response.

Being intentional is different than having an agenda. Of course you want the part (or, if this is a general meeting, you want to be considered for future parts). That's a given. Everyone in the room knows that already. But the meeting can't be "me me me" or the other people feel unseen and unheard. No deal has ever happened without first establishing a relationship.

If you have a big agenda going into the meeting, you are not able to be open. You won't make a connection with anyone. Those meetings aren't about you. They are about the other person. That's how you make a person feel seen.

If you can find a hook to get somebody to connect with you on a personal level, they are going to be more compelled to like you and invest in you. This is what they're asking themselves: Do I like this person? Can I put them on a set? Do I want to invite them into the family that I am going to be living with professionally for the next six months to five years? Do I feel like they could be part of my creative family? Shows are families. A lot of actors are talented. The ones who get jobs are those with whom people personally want to work.

Revisiting headshots

There are a few reasons to revise headshots as you progress in your career.

1 **Your look has changed.** The biggest mistake is sticking with pictures that make you look younger than you are. If you are no longer eighteen but are still trying to play a senior in high school or a college freshman, then you need to look at the shows where those types are being represented and be certain that you can pass for that age authentically. I've seen so many actors in their mid-late twenties still trying to play high-school aged parts. The demeanor, point of view, body language, and self-confidence of an eighteen-year-old is very different than that of a twenty-five-year-old. The journey through college changes you. Living away from home changes a person, too. Play your age. Play what authentically matches your essence and identity. Make sure the pictures you are using reflect that.

2 **A manager or agent asks you to reshoot.** If you sign with representation, many times you will be asked to get new headshots. This is an important conversation that goes back to the understanding of type and vision for your acting career. It is crucial to discuss what the agent doesn't like about your current pictures. (Many of my former students who signed within the first year of graduating were asked to get new pictures. Most of them had just done that in their senior year, for their showcase.) The feedback you receive from the agent or manager will give you information as to how they want to sell you. If that doesn't match with what you see or want, you need to educate them as much as possible. Give them examples of other actresses/actors that have played roles that are right for you. Pay attention if they are mostly contemporary pieces or period pieces. You may be an old soul and your agent/manager doesn't see or get that essence. It's up to you to partner with and educate your reps.

<u>Example</u>

Defining Type for Reshoots, a Case Study

I work with an actress who kept telling me that she saw herself as a "Midge Maisel" type (from the show *The Marvelous Mrs. Maisel*). I told her I didn't see that and she was taken aback. I explained that Rachel Brosnahan was not an actress I would liken her to. I understood what elements of the show she related to, but if I were to give her other types to look at, I would suggest actresses like Lizzy Caplan, Catherine Cohen, and Rachel Bloom. All three are authentically Jewish, are not "typical leading lady" types, and can play a bit older than they are. This is a nuanced conversation to lean into and nailing this kind of specificity will help not only your agents represent you better but guide you toward parts that are right for you.

3 **There is not enough variation in types represented.** You may be asked to take a couple of headshots in scrubs or in a uniform of some kind. There are times when an agent is submitting a new client for a medical show or a specific genre. If they want a picture to show you in that world, take one and see if it gives you traction. As a casting director, I don't need the actual wardrobe in a picture to cast someone, but the tone of the picture is important. You don't need props or anything else other than the simplicity of the wardrobe choice.

Whatever your reason for reshooting headshots, if you are really embracing a certain look and type then don't play it safe. A chance to re-do headshots is the time to fully explore the facets of your personality, style, and energy that belong uniquely to you!

Closing thoughts

Many actors believe they have no entry point into this industry until they have representation. That's simply not true. You can actively (and constantly) seek projects that might be a good fit for you, analyze the breakdowns to better understand how you might be a fit for them, learn how to self-submit so the casting directors will see that fit too, and then knock meetings out of the park when you get them. Most importantly, you have to do this again and again, without giving up. Only those with stamina succeed. I'm sure you've heard the saying: "It's not a sprint, it's a marathon."

8

Head of Creative Development

It's an artist's job to interpret material—and in today's ever changing landscape, it's the artist's job to create material as well.

Actors need content they can use to market themselves effectively. Why not write and shoot something original instead of recycling scenes from movies and past TV scripts? Making original content is also the fastest way to get your work out into the world. When you do it yourself, you take control and create the career you want.

Many times I have students tell me that they are not writers, or that they can't put on a producer, director, or casting hat. They don't see themselves that way. I hear that they want to spend all of their energy trying to audition and get hired as actors because that's what they care about. I want to challenge that mentality. If actors can't think like casting directors, how do they know what to submit for? If actors can't produce, then how are they creating materials to market themselves? If actors aren't directors, then how do they make acting choices within the script that show facets of themselves while honoring the material? In other words, all creatives have some capacity for creative development. It's just not a well exercised muscle for some.

Often, when my students think they can't write, direct, produce, or cast, it's simply because they have a narrow understanding of what it means to "develop content." But developing content could be as simple as making a TikTok or Instagram post!

Your Head of Creative Development will help you take charge of your career, by identifying projects to immerse yourself in that will expand you as an artist and inspire you. This Head will then work with the rest of your board to find the time and resources to actually make it happen. If all goes well, the work will wind up being a good calling card for you as an actor and highlight your other skill sets as well.

Here's what your job as the Head of Creative Development will entail:

- **Find stories.** Develop an original idea or look for something in the media that inspires you.
- **Write, write. Right?** Consult with your boardroom to find time and money, and to get the word out.
- **Choose collaborators.** Your friends, and other up-and-coming creatives have diverse talents. Explore your options.
- **Develop outlines, timelines, and budgets.** You can't build a house without nuts and bolts.
- **Pitch!** Learn how to articulate your vision clearly. Think like a salesperson.

First and foremost, make something you love. Then if there's a great scene of you in it, you can also put it up on Actors Access. But when you create, you showcase more than your talent. You also share your authenticity and passion, and that's what makes people want to work with you.

Find stories

Inspiration comes from so many places. Stories that inspire and compel us have universal themes and truths. And there's no limit to the number of places where you'll find them: in podcasts, magazine and news articles, books, plays, even a little bit of information on social media, not to mention autobiographical material or fictional ideas. Basically, look for depictions of cultural conversations or universal commonalities in this complex and crazy world.

Whatever you work on and develop outside of acting still influences the artist you want to be and creates a conversation surrounding your point of view. If I have a series of journal entries from "the three months I spent back at home as an adult with my parents," that is a story to be developed. Maybe it turns into a monologue. Maybe it becomes a book, maybe it becomes (gasp) a series of Instagram reels! Content is everywhere, waiting to be explored.

Aim to develop something that will meet the industry's current mandates. Although it's hard to know what any particular studio or production company is looking for at any particular time, certain tentpoles are always in demand, for example, female-forward content, YA set in high schools or colleges, BIPOC-centered stories, family dramas, thrillers, romance, contemporary stories, fresh heists, LGBTQIA+ relationship dramas, IP-driven fantasy and sci-fi, and genre-bending comedies.

Also, what role do you intend to play in its creation? Do you want to act, write, produce, or something else? Again, the answers to these questions will help you determine which story is best to pursue first. Consulting your boardroom may give you clues regarding the roles for which you're best suited.

Write, write . . . right?

Once you have determined the sources of inspiration, it's time to develop them, choose one, and start writing. It is not uncommon for creatives to have multiple ideas and stories they want to tell. But how do you determine which projects have real potential, which are relevant to the industry mandates of the time, and which you have the bandwidth to work on? This next part of the process will inform where your interests really lie and if the project is worthy of your time and creative investment.

First, look at each project and give it a title. This can help you determine what that piece will require narratively. For example, if it's "The Day I Lost My Way," then you know you have to lose your way and then come out the other side. Now, explore the full narrative arcs of the projects you're considering. Start by journaling thoughts and impactful phrases from the source material. It can start with a logline for a story. It can start with just a premise. Explore the tangents that develop from there. The source of the story will inform how you proceed.

In some cases, you'll naturally realize that actually you don't want to write a particular piece. You were enamored with the idea or thought it was timely but after exploring it, you change your mind. That's all part of the process! Or maybe you realize it's really more of an aside or a scene within a larger narrative rather than the full narrative itself. Usually you'll know this in the first exploratory phase but sometimes you don't realize this until you've started digging in. I always tell my students it's just as important to know what you **don't** want to write as what you **do** want to write. Developing an idea and starting the writing process will help clarify that.

Once you find something you think you can develop, the next step is to determine its format. Do you want to make a series of short videos to post on Instagram or do you want to make a feature film? Is it a one-act play or solo stage show? Is it a podcast? Think about how much time and money you have to invest in a project. If you find something you love, but you think it would only make sense as a feature film and you don't have the bandwidth right now to try to make a feature film, maybe you pursue that idea later.

I suggest that when first starting out on the writing journey, unless this is a very comfortable process for you, begin with a shortened format: a limited series, short film, short documentary, or similar. This is a good way to flex a muscle that will get stronger over time. I also suggest learning about script structure and investing in screenwriting software, so you may have to check with your CFO regarding budget!

Once you've narrowed down your choices, have a conversation with your entire executive board about whether or not you have the capacity to create this project. If not, maybe there's a different project that will be less intensive (or expensive, time consuming, or whatever your concern is). Finally, research the trades and your network to ensure this is the sort of project that could actually get you attention, based on the industry's current interests/trends.

Now that you're ready, write as robustly as possible. Editing can come later. Identify the central theme with a logline and explore all the various tangents that grow from that. For example, if my logline is: "Kerry is confronted with information from the past that reveals the life she has built is based on secrecy and shameful lies," then Kerry is the protagonist in this story and her obtaining this "information" is the inciting event. Who gave it to her? How did she find it? Who else is involved and what are the stakes if they are revealed? How will it change the course of her life and the lives of others? Where does this take place? In what time period? These are plot builders that will need to be decided upon.

Depending on the type of source material, there may be other considerations. Material can come from myriad places: your own life, other true events, or fiction (including existing intellectual property). Even catch phrases can turn into projects! (My friend made a podcast called "What's Wrong with You People" because she kept hearing herself say that.)

Most young creatives will write something autobiographical or inspired by true events. If it's the former, you're creating the story soup to nuts. If it's the latter, know that stories "based on" a true event will require rights from those who were involved. Stories "inspired" by true events do not. And documentaries require life rights and cooperation from the people involved in that story. If you need to option a piece of media, most authors and playwrights, and even some magazine and news writers, have representation. Start by sleuthing online to learn where the person is repped, and then reach out to ask if the rights are available and what the cost would be to secure them.

The writing process requires time. Your CFO will tell you that time equals money. Look at your schedule and dedicate real time to this process. Slot it in under creative development on a daily, weekly, or bi-monthly basis and use the time dedicated to invest in yourself and your idea. If you need a writing team or accountability, then the next section on choosing collaborators is key. Some creatives do not respond to the solitary nature of writing. It's perfectly fine to know that about yourself and develop strategies that will insure forward movement and success.

Visions of a future, a case study

Every day, I have a student who has a personal story but doesn't know how they'd tell it or even if anyone would be interested. Their proximity to the story paralyzes them and they feel stuck. Here is someone who faced that and came out the other side with an incredible project. The following text is pulled from the program for her solo show.

"In the first week of Fall semester senior year, I met the new Business of Acting/Showcase professor, Wendy Kurtzman. I decided immediately it was important to me for her to get to know the direction I wanted to go in as an actress so that she could help guide my work moving forward; so, we set up an office hour later that week. I expected to enter the conversation and tell her all about my career goals and what kinds of roles I'd played in the past, but that didn't happen. Instead, we talked as people getting to know each other, and I started telling her about my eye history like it was a negative, like it was in the way of my career. She stopped me and asked, "Are you a writer?" I said yes. "You have to tell this story. Listening to you talk about it makes me want to drop everything and help you do it." I was completely stunned. In one day, my invisible, problematic disability became my superpower, and *Tunnel Vision* was born.

"In the beginning I wondered if anyone would care. I always felt like people were tired of hearing about my eyes, about how I don't have peripheral or depth perception. Yeah, we know. But then I remembered the first real conversation I had with a girl in my class freshman year. She told me she couldn't see out of her left eye, which sparked me to tell her how my left is my bad (well, worse) eye too, and then about my eye history. She had never met someone who could relate to her experience, who was her age and really understood what it's like; I could see warmth and a sense of comfort wash over her face as we talked and she realized more and more that I empathized. That girl was Katie Orr, the incredible woman I asked to direct *Tunnel Vision*. Who else? This conversation I had with her four years ago gave me proof that people do care. I have the power to use my life experience to connect with others and stand as an example that it does not define us.

" *Tunnel Vision* has been in the making for nine months. I wrote and rewrote, workshopped, rehearsed, and filmed all with an inspiring group of women on my team. I could never be more grateful for everyone's love and support, and I hope this show inspires you to learn more about Glaucoma and support the cause of finding a cure. Over 60 million people worldwide deserve their vision back. Let's make it happen."

—Bianca Beach

Choose collaborators

Seeking collaborators for your project requires the skills of the CEO. The vision you have will be best served by those who share equally in your passion. If you are running the project like a CEO, consistency is the priority and choosing reliable collaborators will be of utmost importance. When you start a project like this, you become a producer. Your new project is no different than any other project in development: you need to find people to fill in all of the roles you can't do yourself. Maybe you want someone else to write it, or to write it with you. Maybe you want someone else to produce it behind the scenes, or maybe you just need financing.

How many collaborators you'll need will depend on how many skills you have within your own wheelhouse. However, only pull on as many collaborators as you'll absolutely need, especially in the beginning. Development periods are long. People's plans sometimes change along the way. Your plans may change!

Especially for young artists starting out, they usually lean on their classmates or people from their acting community. This is a time to call on your posse, and for that matter, you should make yourself available when your posse calls on you—it's a two-way street. The challenge in this is that most emerging artists are opportunistic and focused on their own objectives, so when you choose your collaborators, you need to be very clear what your expectations are and what role you expect your fellow collaborators to play. If you outline a project and it is heavily dependent on a specific person's contribution or availability, it is important to create a contract or working understanding of that time commitment and what that job will be. Be specific and create professional boundaries. If you are relying on trading free equipment for exposure in the film or bartering your skill set for someone else's involvement, understand that there needs to be a Plan B if your initial choices of collaborators become unavailable. Create a contingency plan to pivot to with research and intention before you start.

A producer is a juggler with lots of balls in the air at one time. The job requires working all aspects simultaneously and not letting a single ball drop.

Develop outlines, timelines, and budgets

I cannot stress enough how important it is that you actually do create outlines, timelines, and budgets. Legitimize this process by treating it as a professional endeavor. Think of the questions you will be asked once it's up and running. Sometimes, once you sit down and really wrestle with some of these questions, you may find out your goals aren't actually realistic within the set parameters and you'll need to adjust the scope of the project. Maybe you'll need more money than you thought. Or maybe you'll need more or fewer people than you reached out to initially.

Talk doesn't turn into action. If you really are working on something creative, then you must carve time out to honor that creative development and make it happen. No one is going to give you time to sit down and write your script or make the edits or changes unless you say, "I'm sorry I can't do anything today, I'm working on the rewrite of my script." If you don't have an agent or publisher imposing a deadline, then you have to impose those deadlines and set those goals yourself. Honor it, carve time out for it, create an outline and budget around it. Make it real. Don't just say, I'm doing it. This business demands specificity. I cannot stress that enough. As an actor, you already know the importance of bringing specificity to the choices you make in a scene. They speak to the characters' emotions, motivations, struggles, and secrets. You have to bring the same kind of specificity to every other aspect of this career. Anyone can come up with an idea. Only those who implement ideas succeed.

If you are serious about developing a project, go to breakdown services, and look at the breakdowns for projects similar to yours. That can be a helpful template. Get access to itemized budgets for projects, either from Studio Binder, or friends or mentors, and start to hash out what your budget will be. Think about how much money you're planning to spend—if you aren't going to have enough, you either need to consider new forms of financing, or you need to shift the project (maybe it's a web series instead of a film, or maybe you shoot it in your apartment instead of city streets, which would require a permit). Financing for a project is an inevitable imperative. Consider researching crowdsourcing platforms such as: GoFundMe, Kickstarter, Indiegogo, and Seed & Spark. Studio Binder also contains helpful information about obtaining grants and provides other resources surrounding the production process.

When you create a detailed outline, that allows you to create specific budgets and timelines. Then, you can fill in your creative team. If that team reaches beyond your student posse then be prepared to create a proposal that's specific to each creative role involved. The more you can articulate the scope of your project and the creative support you are seeking, the more you will be a successful producer and creator. Don't just rely on a handshake with friends. They too have objectives and opportunities they are seeking as well and may not be available when you need them.

Pitch

Creating an effective pitch is a very large part of the creative process. Further, in order to articulate the story and ideas you have for your project, you will need some visual materials. These can be as simple as a one-sheet and synopsis or as developed as a pitch deck or even a sizzle. What's most important is to find a way to communicate your concept in a succinct and engaging manner. Remember all those different hats you are capable of wearing—writer, director, producer, casting director? Your multi-hyphenate is really called into action during the pitch process.

Now that you've begun developing the idea you want to create, your next step will be to create a visual or a one-sheet that includes your overall logline. For instance, if my project is about "a father and son who find each other after a lifetime apart," then I might start with some pictures of those two characters embracing or possibly shaking hands for the first time. I might pull pictures of a young man waiting in a café. I might include a picture of a letter, with the text, "Dear son" at the top. If my story has a specific geographical location or belongs in a certain era, my materials can reflect those aspects as well. One great resource for such visuals can be found at shotdeck.com.

If the aspects of the story are already flushed out and there's an outline, write a synopsis. This will be a chance to introduce the main characters and the story arc. It will provide a window into the obstacles and challenges the characters face. Whatever it is you're developing, ask yourself, "What can I create to help pitch my concept?"

If you are a good editor, or know a friend who is, then you can create a sizzle reel. This can be done with clips, captions, and music. It's for concept only—to create tone, sense of place, and incorporate the sounds and voices of the characters. Conversely, static images and art along with a logline and story synopsis will make an effective pitch deck. Search online for a YouTube converter for help adding clips to sizzles.

Pitches are pieces of your imagination and artistry. They can become points of discussion at any time. Someone may see them on your website, LinkedIn profile, or Instagram and be intrigued by the conversation you have started. They may want to collaborate or finance a piece of it. At the least, they will admire you for creating. Your pitches not only show more creativity—they show initiative, vision, and action. Someone with those attributes is someone people want to work with. That's what development does for you. So open up your mind to the "you" who is a multi-faceted creative. None of us is just one thing. The world out there is waiting.

Closing thoughts: Make and share

Now make the damn thing! And enjoy the process. Your Head of Creative Development is there to help you create content not only to further your career, but also to give you opportunities to indulge in the creative process and remember why you chose this industry in the first place. The industry is looking for people who are willing to risk and do the work.

The most compelling reason to lean into creative development is that it can give you something to look forward to that's within your control and exciting when you're not auditioning. It should be the thing you can't wait to get back to as soon as your self-tape or callback is over.

9

Head of Outreach

Give with no agenda. Why am I telling you, in a book about acting, to give with no agenda? First of all, it's good advice, regardless of the topic of this book. Second, you can only bring experience, knowledge, and perspective to your work when you indulge a broader sensibility, open yourself to experiences, or share a passion as a human being.

I'll never forget a phone call I received from a veteran talent agent after a symposium we had done together. She told me that she observed that the students' singular focus on getting a job was uninteresting and ultimately made them forgettable. "It's not about the job, it's about who you are," she told me, referencing the criteria she uses when looking for actors to represent or collaborate with. "It's about the life you lead, not the job you want."

Helping your career is not the main reason to do for others and live a full life, of course, but it is a damn nice side effect. Outreach is about everything but you. Only when you turn outward can you grow inward. Whenever I meet students who aren't dedicating part of their lives to nurturing others and themselves, I give them the advice you are about to read. The feedback coming back to me is always, "Holy shit, you were right."

Outreach changes you as a person and puts a different perspective on so many pieces of this business. It gets you out of your cycle of need. It's important to create something that's uniquely yours and that has power outside of the paradigm of need, because that paradigm is destructive and narrow.

Outreach opens you up, expands you. As a result, it changes your relationship with your work: the dynamic in meetings, correspondence with contacts, and expectations throughout. Sometimes we are so hyperfocused on getting what we want that we forget to just be a person. Your Head of Outreach has three main duties.

- **Volunteer.** Help others, full stop.
- **Indulge a hobby.** Explore an interest completely unrelated to acting or story.
- **Connect people.** Help friends and contacts, within or outside the industry.

Even if outreach yields nothing beneficial for your career, it will change you for the better, and you'll never regret the investment.

Volunteer

I don't need to tell you why it's important to do things for other people without asking for anything in return. You've been hearing it from your parents, your religious institutions, and/or your school for years. But I can tell you about some of the lovely benefits it will have on your career.

Think about it: People who are absorbed in themselves are completely uninteresting. We are not drawn to those people. In short time, we avoid them. Either they talk about nothing but the industry or, worse, they speak only of themselves. No one will want to work with you if you're completely self-absorbed. Rather, we are attracted to people who are passionate about others. You will like yourself more when you volunteer.

Also, it is only when you turn outward that you have revelations about your career and about yourself. If you are always asking, "What do I get from this?" then you're not open to the experience. You want to train yourself to approach things without an agenda, which volunteering inherently helps you do. Don't just do it to post on Instagram. Do it to help you grow.

Dogged pursuits, a case study

A former student of mine discovered a unique form of outreach that combines her skills as a writer with something she loves . . . dogs!

"If there is one thing about me, it's that I will stop on the street any time I see a dog to say hello. It consistently brings a smile to my face and makes my day a little bit brighter. As I like to say, 'there is nothing better than telling a dog how cute they are to boost their ego.' I always grew up with a dog in my house (which I took for granted), but I never realized just how much I loved them until my family rescued a dog in 2020, shortly after my childhood dog passed away. From the moment I met my new furry best friend, I was smitten. He brought indescribable joy into my life at a time I needed it most—being sent home from my BFA program early due to COVID.

I have known Wendy since I was 16 years old, and among the many, many life lessons I have learned from her over the years, one of the most crucial is the emphasis she places on connection and outreach in stepping outside of yourself as an artist. I've always enjoyed the act of connecting people, recommending friends for jobs, and playing matchmaker, so I thought my outreach was set and done. But, in applying Wendy's model as a means of creating more structure for myself post-grad, I realized that one element of my life that was somewhat lacking was a different kind of outreach. Coincidentally, around one of the many times Wendy and I were discussing the challenges I was facing as an actor fresh out of a BFA program, a friend who is involved at a local dog rescue told me about their volunteer programs. At this rescue, they were in need of general volunteers and people to help write Instagram bios for dogs to capture their personalities in hopes that potential adopters would come meet them in person. I was hooked. It sounded exactly like something that I would want to do, and could maybe even be good at.

It turns out that this kind of outreach was a missing puzzle piece that allowed me to find a way to step outside of myself, help dogs find their forever homes, and use my skills as a writer for good. Once I went through the process of rescuing my family dog, I knew it was a cause I wanted to support in my adult life. There is no better feeling than going to the rescue, playing with a dog in the yard, and making them more adoptable day by day. I could play with a dog for twenty minutes, which spreads joy to both parties, then use my observational skills as an actor to gauge their personality and turn on my writer brain to think of witty and creative ways to showcase them on social media. This kind of volunteer work became a perfect marriage of using my creative skills for good and my love of dogs. Based on what's needed, I don't always write a bio when I volunteer, but there is so much joy in putting my energy toward the needs of the organization. Knowing I can show up when I can, put all of my life stuff aside and make one dog just a smidge more adoptable, I can take five seconds to not think about myself.

The world of a multi-hyphenate can often be a lonely one. It feels like you are constantly putting your efforts into a void. Despite being surrounded by people, whether it be fellow employees at side hustles or the entire community full of people wanting you to succeed, you must find the motivation within yourself to pursue the craft day after day. That requires a lot of introspection, and by taking the time to look inward, you are expending such a unique form of energy that can be really draining. So, by taking the time to step outside of yourself entirely, put 'I' to the side, and put a little bit of energy toward something you care about other than your craft, you might find an increased sense of purpose, adding more fuel to your creative fire. As artists, we need to experience life beyond art. Sure, this method of outreach uses creative skills, but I'm not doing it to benefit my career in any way. It is actually a way for me to exercise creativity without any pressure of an industry end goal. The end goal is much bigger—for me, it's to foster my passion for helping dogs over the course of my adult life. Combined with a quality HR department (I find these two often work hand in hand for your mental health), you can make outreach more than just a good deed or a box to check, you can use it as a tool for a more fulfilling life."

—Isabel Wynne

Indulge a hobby

Remember Hannah Gadsby's Netflix special? She talks a lot about her background in Art History. What struck me about this was that she used it in her routine, and was incredibly interesting and knowledgeable in a refreshing and unorthodox way. She regaled the audience with pieces of history that colored my perception of Van Gough and Picasso in ways I hadn't been exposed to or previously discussed. I was intellectually drawn to her and interested in her as a human being. The performer part was secondary, as if it were merely a fortuitous platform on which she could share this information.

I tell this story because we are all interesting in other ways. We all have passions and opinions. Honor and share the pieces of yourself that are tied to your values, your interests and self worth. This is what makes us unique. This makes us interesting. This makes us attractive.

How can you be a truly effective artist if you haven't explored these sides of yourself? Additionally, stories live in these experiences. Human interest stories, historical stories, love stories. And who is better to tell them, develop them, create them, than someone with an artistic soul? The only criteria for getting involved in any number of these opportunities is you must enter into these experiences—with no agenda, with just an open mind and an open heart.

Passion and purpose

Here's a short list of some suggested ways you can get outside of yourself, either by volunteering, picking up a hobby, or doing something that's both:

Politics
Religion/faith
LGBTQIA+ causes
Black Lives Matter and/or BIPOC organizations
Women's rights
Storytelling
Environmental activism
Art
Music
Poetry
Food and shelter organizations
Veterans resources and education
Cooking/nutrition
Advocacy for alternately abled individuals
Health-related organizations
Lecture series
Book clubs
Animal shelters
Outreach departments through artistic organizations.

Teach and be taught, a case study

Here's another story from a former student about the incredible benefits of outreach.

"As a young black actress, I took a lot of the concepts of outreach to heart. I was specifically excited when the idea was introduced to me professionally because it was something I had already integrated into my life. I took the outreach route to expand my abilities as a storyteller while also serving my community. It expanded my life experiences, opportunities, and childlike imagination. Outreach made me more empathetic and more interesting to talk to. It may not seem important when all you want to be is an actor for hire. As hard as it is to even get one acting job, you probably doubt the necessity to focus on anything but the craft itself. However, when I started thinking of myself as a business, with both responsibility for and the need of the community, I became a better actress—a more complete artist.

"Stories are something we all are introduced to as a child. We read them in books, watched them on TV, and even created our own in make-believe games. While we each fell in love with them in different ways, the impact stories had on our imagination as children are priceless. They are so valuable in fact, that as a professional storyteller, it is essential for you to return to your childlike place. So, what do you do if you don't know how?

"As an actress, I have been fortunate to have formally trained since the age of ten. This allowed me to have a deep appreciation for words and the imagination of others. But somewhere in the midst of being an orphan, my ambitions to create a career for myself, and essentially the idolization of being 'grown up,' my childhood was cut short. So, when I got to college to receive my BFA in Acting and every teacher had the same note, 'You need to open up and play more,' I knew there was only one way to do it. I had to learn from kids how to see the world like a kid, so that I could remember what it felt like to be a kid. Because who else plays better than kids?

"I want to say that at the time I thought long and hard about which age group has the most fruitful imagination before I started working with children on this. But the truth is, the CFO of my company said I simply needed a flexible minimum wage job to help me get through college. As a fellow artist, I'm sure you can relate. However, this job ended up being a preschool teacher's assistant through Americorps. It was both a community service and a work position. I couldn't have been luckier.

"In a *Scholastic* article titled, 'Creative Development in 3–5 Year Olds,' Michelle Anthony, PhD, writes, 'The world of the preschooler is one of imagination and magic. Many children will reach their creative peak before the age of six, after which it will begin to decline due to formal schooling and the developmental drive towards conformity.' Sound familiar? Anthony went on to explain how the creativity and imagination formed in these early years will inadvertently affect your abilities throughout adulthood. By the age of three, a child has entered 'Piaget's Preoperational Period.' They begin to create from their imagination intentionally, such as purposefully drawing a dog or a flower because they imagined what it would look like. By age five, they have the ability to create in detail, often narrating to friends or family the story behind the picture they drew.

"As a teacher's assistant my job was to aid in giving more individualized attention than one teacher would allow. These were kids who had a tough life already. These preschools were located in the basements of public-housing projects throughout New York City. It felt good as a college student to help a four-year-old laugh and make crafts, especially when they had no food or toys at home. This also allowed me to observe each child in detail: their behavioral patterns, their social skills, and most importantly, their association of what they are learning to what they have seen in the world or imagined in their mind. All of this has direct correlation to the techniques we learn on character development in drama school.

"A primary example of this came when I monitored the dramatic-play area during free time. Billy was alone cooking at the play kitchen, lonely and bored. I watched him construct a plan to get the others to come play with him: an objective. A light bulb went off and he yelled, 'FIIIIRE.' Suddenly five girls and boys hurried from the coloring area to the dramatic station to gear up in fire-fighter suits. They gathered toy cups, plates, and even toy food, and rushed to the stove to put out the imaginary fire. I saw them panting as if battling fear, labor, and adrenaline. I watched them pretend the cups were filled with water as they splashed the fire out one by one. I saw them look around, talking to each other as they collectively understood this was not a one-kid job. They continued in this high-stakes scenario until they had all 'seen' the fire go out, at which point their attention switched to something new.

> "There is so much one can relate here to the fundamentals of storytelling or acting. However, the overall message is that I learned just as much from those kids as they learned from me. I worked with underprivileged children for over five years. Embracing the outreach department of my business allowed me to use my education and talents to make an impact on someone's life—something every storyteller strives for. But it also enriched that very talent and gave me the knowledge I needed to expand my company as a whole."
>
> —Rae'l Ba

Connect people

Be a connector! Introduce people you admire to other people you admire, either because you think they might collaborate with one another by filling each other's professional and artistic needs, or simply because you think they might like each other. Play matchmaker and also be the sort of person who is the hub for get togethers, mixers—and not just for industry people.

You don't know where it's going to lead, that's the point. That's why it's not mercenary. The idea of having a crew is that you support these people and you're all building something together. Maybe you'll scratch each other's backs later, maybe not. The point is that you are all engaging in a larger conversation.

Take the idea of outreach and build community. You can collaborate with those beyond the entertainment industry. You don't have to just focus on connecting individuals that will lead to something you are directly involved with. If two people you connected wind up collaborating together successfully, it will circle back to you. You don't always have to place yourself in the middle of every conversation.

"Let me introduce you to," a case study

A young actress I know, Alex, told me a story that I think is an excellent example of playing matchmaker for friends and fellow creatives without any agenda. A playwright friend of hers reached out to a group with a specific breakdown of a play she wrote that was receiving a staged reading. The playwright's breakdown mentioned the character's specs and that they needed an actress with exceptional comedic timing. Upon reading the breakdown, Alex immediately thought, "I have someone! And she's perfect!" Alex reached out to the actress to gauge her interest and availability, and once she confirmed, Alex coordinated the actress passing her materials along to the playwright. It was then out of her hands and into those of her friend auditioning for the part, but she was overjoyed to learn from the playwright that the actress booked the role in the reading. She was able to go and watch both of her friends succeed on the night of the reading, and watch them not only become collaborators, but develop a friendship.

This actress connected with no agenda of her own. She knew there was no role in her for this project, nothing for her to get out of it in service of career. It is a prime example of playing matchmaker in a way that celebrates and boosts the creative success of others. Sure, it can often feel like a competitive numbers game, but when you put that kind of no-agenda, giving energy out in the world, hopefully it will come back to you in return.

Another great example of connecting others comes from a former student, who took an interesting connection all the way to a week long job, and later even an audition opportunity. One day, Sam was contacted by another friend in the industry asking if he was interested in working on the set of a film in a capacity he had no experience working in. Sam took the interview not expecting much of it, realized he probably wasn't right for this specific role, and pitched himself to work in another capacity for the duration of the shoot. To make a long story short, the creative team took him on in a different role! He was able to spend a full week on set learning, observing, and connecting with the cast, crew, and creative team. From standing directly behind the director's monitor to learning from the 2nd AD, he was able to experience first hand what happens on the other side of the camera. In meeting the producers, Sam mentioned he was an actor, and they passed his materials along to casting, who actually called him in to audition for a film. He is able to trace back all of the connections he made, relationships he built, and even an audition back to his original connection given without expecting anything in return. They provided an opportunity for someone else to learn and grow, and by doing so, allowed this young actor to open up his network.

Closing thoughts

Do for others by volunteering and connecting. Enrich your life through volunteer work and hobbies. This will remind you of what you care about and who you are as a person. It will fulfill you in ways your profession cannot. It will have an impact on you as a person and as a creator that will benefit your profession in unique and profound ways.

10

Putting It All Together

Remember a colleague of mine once said the biggest challenge artists face is when they sit at the kitchen table and say to themselves, "It's Tuesday at 11am—what now?" This perfectly encapsulates the overwhelm that results from lack of structure. When you have dozens of things to do, and they're all a little different from each other, and nothing has been assigned to you since everything is self started, it can feel impossible to do anything at all.

When you create a boardroom for your creative career, and designate tasks to different seats at the table, you give yourself the gift of structure. Then, you'll sit down on Tuesday at 11am and say, "My Head of Biz Development has about 30 minutes of updating to do in my contacts list. My Head of Creative Development wanted to start working out the budget for that comedy sketch I'm making for my acting reel. My outreach department needs me to drop off those resources for Habitat for Humanity. Since I was up late last night finishing the outline for that Instagram Reels sketch, I know my head of HR will demand I budget in some self-care."

Now that you know all of the different seats at your boardroom table, as well as every duty each is responsible for, it will be easy to know what tasks need to be accomplished. Sit with your CEO to organize those tasks anyway you like. Many of my students prefer to make color-coded lists, one per board seat. Then they pull out their calendars, and literally write in different tasks on different days. Honestly, it doesn't matter what kind of calendar or time-management system you use, as long as you use one.

Sometimes you'll stay on one objective for a whole week. That's fine, as long as you make a plan for when you'll get back to the needs of the other boardroom seats. There will also be times when priorities shift or an emergency arises, requiring you to pivot and re-organize your calendar. That's all part of it. As long as you're not ignoring any of the seats at your table, then you are doing it right!

As a creative you will want to have your hand in everything. Unless you really carve out time for specific tasks and give yourself permission to indulge those objectives, you won't actually do them. That process requires difficult prioritizing decisions, the kind you may never have been challenged to make before. When you cultivate and utilize your boardroom, when it becomes a tangible and visual model, the behind-the-scenes processes become much more manageable and clear. At that point, anything is possible. The sky is the limit.

The other incredible benefit to this system is accountability. Are you more inclined to show up for a workout session if you've prepaid for it? Are you more likely to attend a workshop if there's a non-refundable deposit? Interestingly, when there is a financial consequence, the prioritizing is very clear. Train yourself to look at accountability to yourself and your career as an equal investment.

So go draw up your table! The components exemplified in each seat are all already within us. But we don't always listen to them. When you give them "Department Head" titles, you endorse them and their value. On the following pages, you will find a sample calendar for reference. To get a more dynamic view, please consult the online resources, where this calendar is color coded. In this way, you recognize those facets of yourself and create space for your priorities.

Acknowledge every side of yourself: it's part of how you become a fully realized artist! Once that happens, you are free to achieve your dreams.

WEEK AT A GLANCE:

	SUN	MON	TUES	WED
9 AM		Trades/Podcast Research (BIZ DEV)		Morning Workout/ Meditation (HR)
10 AM	Morning Hike (HR)		Morning Workout/ Meditation (HR)	Audition Prep (REP)
11 AM		Schedule/Prep for Zoom Script Session (CREATIVE DEV)		
12 PM				
1 PM	Social Media Reach Out (M&B)			Self Tape: Set Up, Edit, Submit (REP)
2 PM		Rep Meeting (REP)	Audition Prep (REP)	
3 PM				
4 PM				Update Website/Pos Materials (M&B)
5 PM	Rep Meeting Prep (REP)			
6 PM		Work Shift (CFO)	Work Shift (CFO)	
7 PM	Weekly Meal Prep (CFO)			
8 PM				
9 PM				Watch Two New F (BIZ DEV)
10 PM				

Putting It All Together: Sample Schedule. See color-coded and fully labeled version online.

SAMPLE CALENDAR

THURS	FRI	SAT
Zoom Script Session (CREATIVE DEV)	Trades/Podcast Research (BIZ DEV)	
	Morning Workout/Meditation (HR)	Volunteer (OUTREACH)
Work Shift (CFO)	Work Shift (CFO)	Improv Class (CREATIVE DEV)
Industry Mixer (BIZ DEV)	Dinner with Friends (HR)	Movie Trivia Night (HR)

Part II

Industry Insights

11

Casting FAQ

Over the years, at countless symposiums and panels, my colleagues and I have answered actors' burning questions. Here, I have gathered the ones most frequently asked. Each response represents the current consensus in our field.

Q: Let's talk about what makes a strong online audition and identify some of the components that will help . . . ie., background, lighting, costumes, sound, props. Since these are being done at home and in apartments, should actors try to make readings feel more life-like or should they still feel like a self-tape atmosphere?

A: The most important aspect of a self tape is the work itself. To complement that, the audio and lighting are also a priority. We need to see and hear you clearly. There are many resources online that identify the best practices for self-tape, but casting directors don't need or expect a professionally produced self-tape. We understand the constraints that actors work under and are generous when it comes to at-home situations that don't allow for complete privacy and or sound proofing. Do your best. Again, it's about the work. If there is a way to add minimal production value to the tape that is fine, but nothing that will distract from the work. Having strong eye lines is a consideration as well. Think about who's in the scene—who should be getting your focus and who is distracting you.

Q: What are the common factors that keep an actor from getting a role? Other than maybe being a wrong type or having a different look than imagined. Are there positives or negatives that stand out to you?

A: Two big contributing factors are being unprepared or not making strong choices based on the information in the script. It's not just about identifying the emotions tied to the scene but how those emotions are disrupted when you are not achieving your objective. Listening is just as important, if not more so, than talking.

Q: Should an actor ask questions about the circumstances or the set-up before an audition (if they have not seen a script)? Would you give them time to digest this info or is it best to just make a choice and hope to get redirected if it's wrong?

A: Yes, it's okay to request clarification if you think getting it will help you develop a stronger point of view. Most actors need time to digest new information, so they can make actionable choices in the scene. If that's the case, then it's best to ask for some time and to let other actors go ahead until the information can be digested and processed.

Q: If there is a redirect in the room, can an actor take time to digest this info or are they expected to perform immediately? If they want more time how does that weigh on their chances to be cast?

A: If you understand a redirect and it's easily implemented, go-ahead and play with it right away. Otherwise, seek clarity first. It's important to understand the intention behind the redirect. For example, if you are asked to play the scene "stronger or with more force," should you interpret that as anger, frustration, or resentment? Try restating it back in the form of a statement. "So, I am angry at them for putting me in this position," or "I am frustrated that I can't get out of this situation," or "I resent being put in this situation." Then, if the CD concurs, you know you are both on the same page. If not, it will allow the CD to re-articulate.

Q: What are the best ways for actors to ensure their work is seen?

A: Hands down, the best way to get your work seen is to create your own content and market it or through an audition request from a casting director. Self-tapes for projects are watched, if requested. In addition, pay attention to industry-driven initiatives such as CSA (Casting Society) open calls.

Q: There is a lot of talk about actors developing additional skills and training as a way to increase their hireability. What are some of the things you appreciate or lean into?

A: Improvisation, physical skills, mastering accents and languages, and any "special skill" that is unique or unexpected.

Q: What is the relationship between the CD and the actor? Are actors encouraged to reach out via DM, FB Messenger, email, or the telephone? Do CDs respond to clips attached to correspondence?

A: It's entirely appropriate to maintain a healthy business relationship with industry professionals. Respect boundaries and reach out when there is something concrete to share. Make sure the correspondence is not just about what you want, but that it also "gives" to your fellow professional, for example, by congratulating them on a recent award or nomination, or by recognizing their work in some way. The response to the correspondence depends on timing. If we have something and your message has jogged our memory, we will respond. If we don't respond, we still appreciate hearing from you and your efforts to maintain a connection. Trust that if you have auditioned before that you will be remembered in the future if you had a strong audition. Casting directors keep notes on auditions and refer to them on subsequent projects.

Q: What's the best piece of advice you give to aspiring actors?

A: See casting directors as your collaborators. They want you to do well and succeed. Use the time in the audition room as a chance to share who you are, what you do, and why you find joy in your craft. We love being in the room with you (both in person and when watching your work virtually). Our job is to shepherd people and get them hired. We are all in this together.

12

Interviews: Let's Get Down to Business

Casting professionals

Michael Sanford, CSA, CCDA Casting Director, Sanford Casting

Michael Sanford Casting opened in the spring of 2000 as primarily a commercial casting company. He and his team worked with many top directors, production companies, and advertising agencies to create an actor and client-friendly office bringing thousands of commercial campaigns to life. In 2009 he expanded into a full service casting company to include feature films, television, theatre, music videos, digital content and more. In 2018 he partnered with Jillian Johnston who is based in Atlanta to open a southeast office, Sanford Johnston Casting. He has been awarded a CSA Artios Award for his work on the Oscar winning film *The Artist* alongside his friend and mentor Heidi Levitt, a TMA Heller Award for Commercial Casting Director of the Year, and a Media Access Award for his work with the Casting Society of America's Equity in Entertainment Committee.

A closer look at commercial casting

Wendy: How do actors prepare for a commercial audition? Do they have copy and context ahead of time and how do they know the "tone" of the commercial?

Michael: When a commercial has copy, we'll send the script in advance of the audition and include all relevant notes about the character, tone, and style of the spot. We'll also include the storyboards if we're able to. Often times, talent or their agents will have to sign an NDA beforehand. If the commercial has no dialogue we'll post everything in the waiting room prior to talent coming in. My lobby assistant will also give group explanations and we'll generally go over it again in the room before the audition. If it's a self tape audition we'll send all relevant information and instructions to the actor or their agent beforehand when we send the audition request.

W: Who is normally in a commercial casting session? Are the clients there from the start?

M: First calls are generally myself and a session director and assistant. Commercial turnaround times are often so fast that I can't always be in the room as I'm prepping the actors for the next day or I might have multiple sessions going. Because of this we have TV monitors in our office so I can see what's going on in each room and can dialogue with my team virtually in the event I need them to make adjustments. It's at the callback when the director and ad agency/client are also present. If the first call is online it's generally myself and my operator. When it's an online callback it's my entire team along with the director, producer, and ad agency. They all generally have their cameras shut off while the actor performs and the director or myself will pop on after the take to give adjustments.

W: What are some of the common pitfalls in a commercial casting audition? For example, overselling? Too much movement?

M: Yes, both of those examples you mentioned actually. "Less is more" has become a new general note in commercials so actors don't need to over emphasize anything with the dialogue, their reactions, and especially when saying the name of the product. The general tone is to keep everything very conversational as if you're talking to a best friend. In addition to too much movement not enough movement can also be a pitfall depending on how we're framing the shot. For example, if we frame you from your waist up you will have more freedom of movement than if we frame you in a close-up shot say from shoulders up. So that same amount of movement on this tighter take might pull you out of frame. It's important that actors take an on-camera commercial technique class as this process is very different from that of film or television auditions.

W: What are the technical "musts" for an effective commercials audition, e.g. camera frame, lighting, sound, wardrobe, etc.?

M: All of those. However, much of that is our responsibility to control at the audition studio such as the lighting, sound quality, and framing. The example I gave above around framing is something my session operator will adjust in the room but with so many auditions being self-tapes now, much of this is now on the actor. So we'll always include very specific instructions when we send the audition notice, i.e. record against a solid background if possible, frame yourself in a close-up for the slate, then a mid-shot for the action, if you're recording on your phone, flip it sideways so it's in landscape mode giving us a full frame video, etc. We'll outline this step by step on the self-tape instruction sheet.

W: Should an actor dress as the profession when auditioning for a commercial?

M: It will change with every audition but we'll give talent the necessary wardrobe notes. For example we'll say dress casual, or perhaps we ask them to wear a business suit if the character is an executive or perhaps upscale casual if it's something in between. We'll provide this both with the audition request and on the instruction sheet. It's not necessary though for an actor to spend extra money on different types of uniforms, i.e. scrubs or a lab coat for medical roles. We might indicate that if you have those please wear them but if not dressing casual is fine. It still is going to come down to the best person for the job and wardrobe will ultimately be provided for them.

W: Headshots: Is there still a need to have a "commercial" headshot? If yes, what is the most effective look and style?

M: Back "in the day" a commercial headshot was often one that had a big smile or was very energetic. Commercials in general have become so much more natural in tone so the main shot should invoke a sense of warmth and/or your essence. This usually comes from the eyes. Nothing should be staged or posed and actors shouldn't be holding any props in the shot. Think of commercials now as 30-second short films. Actors can have more fun or have specific character-type headshots posted on the casting site, but your main one should be neutral and direct.

W: How often do you check social media and other sources when casting for a commercial?

M: We check them often but not so much for the amount of followers someone has but more for what people are like in their everyday lives to get a sense of them. This is particularly helpful when someone doesn't have any footage yet. Advertising clients will often have us check social media accounts to be sure there is nothing controversial posted on an actor's account, especially if they're going to be representing a brand. We'll also occasionally post a breakdown on our business social media page especially if we're looking for something specific that we might not find through the traditional casting databases.

W: What are some of the ways you give actors a sense of security or comfort when they come in for an audition?

M: We love actors and pride ourselves on being an actor-friendly office. We keep the entire environment from sign-in to audition professional but casual. We'll talk with the actors before we begin so they know they're welcome, answer any questions about the material, and will always give them a run through, rehearsal, and most likely at least one adjustment. The adjustment is to see how well they take it for our clients but also for us to get a sense of their range. If there's no dialogue in a spot and it's a reaction or quick cut to their face for a moment we might do a personality slate on camera for the client can get to know them a little. This is generally to tell us one fun or interesting about them that has nothing to do with showbusiness,

W: What if the commercial suggests that an actor is engaged in an activity? Like throwing a baseball, drinking coffee, etc. Should the actor bring in a prop?

M: If props are needed we generally provide them or will ask actors to bring them if it's specific or personal, for example, a toothbrush or hairbrush. If we have to see a special ability or skill such as throwing a baseball, many actors have that footage on their resumés under what are called skill clips. We've also held sessions or callbacks outside the studio at a park or baseball field for example. We needed actors who were also runners a few weeks back for a comedy spot. During the self-tape process we asked them to record their dialogue and reactions inside, then go outside to a park or safe place to get 10–20 seconds of them running. We got some wonderful and fun footage on that one.

W: How often do you keep actors in mind for other commercials when they are not what the client wants but did a good job?

M: 100percent of the time. We keep very detailed notes and databases.

W: Is it appropriate for actors to "stay in touch"? If yes, how do you prefer they do that?

M: Yes, we have an email for actors: msanfordcasting@gmail.com. We might not be able to return them all but we do go through them all. Actors can also follow us on our social media business account. We also still go through our mail but aren't fans of sending 8×10's as we can access those online but instead send a postcard with what you've been up to, how can we find your info online, etc.

Carol Dudley, CSA, CDG, Producer/Casting Director

Carol Dudley began her career in Los Angeles with Reuben Cannon before moving to London in the early 90s. She has extensive casting credits, and, now, producer credits, with *The Laureate* set to debut in cinemas in the US, *Slammer*, a low budget sci-fi film in post, as well as "Books & Drinks." Carol is a member of the CSA European branch and a member of CDG, BAFTA and ATAS.

"The British invasion" and what the Brits know that we don't

Wendy: Let's talk about your career choice to move to the UK at the height of your success in casting here in the US. I don't really know many casting directors who had a robust career in the States, trained here and then picked up and moved "across the pond." It gives you a unique way to look at the business and the casting world from two distinct vantage points. I know you left around 1990 . . . why?

Carol: Because of the Berlin Wall coming down and I had this "cockamamie" idea in my head that somehow there'd be all these bottled-up stories in Eastern Europe that would get free. I wanted to be where the new stories were coming out. I also had seen the series "Flickers" with Bob Hoskins and Frances de la Tour. It was about the early days of filmmaking, hence the title "Flickers" and I thought, the great thing is in England, they cast Frances de la Tour who's not the American ideal of a leading lady. In the US, we'd have cast someone like Jessica Lange, they would've put her in a frumpy sweater and with her hair parted in the middle, looking horrible and then as the character fell in love, she would transform into Jessica. Like it was against the law for anybody who's not drop-dead gorgeous to have a love life! And that's what I had observed about everybody, especially on television, right? At the time, there were so many people who looked like each other.

W: So it was just knowing that you could cast much more interesting people because England's audience would buy it?

C: Yes. These shows won a lot of awards and Frances de la Tour is probably the best-known character actress in England for both comedy and drama.

W: Why do you think that the look of the actors that were working in film and TV then were so different? Do you think it was influenced by the fact that there's such a large amount of British theatre and the criteria for theatre just kind of seeped over into the television world?

C: Because everybody did everything. You know, you didn't have "TV actors" and "film actors" and "theatre actors." Everybody started in the theatre. You had all the repertory companies and actors went to the Royal Shakespeare Company or they went to a repertory company. That's how they learned their first professional skills. They were already trained. You were brought up to respect the older actors, and everybody wanted to be an actor. They didn't want to be a celebrity. They didn't want to be a star. And if you said those words, it was like instantly, "you are totally uncool." Also, in the States, you have economic uncertainty, whereas the people who leave the drama schools go into established institutions where they get a weekly paycheck. The UK fosters a working class of actors.

W: So when you say the established institutions are you meaning the National Theatre, Royal Shakespeare Company, Birmingham Rep, Manchester Rep ... all of the out-of-town theatres?

C: Yes. You have older actors there, who teach, and you don't have the economic uncertainty. You might be getting modest pay, but you're generally getting your housing and a weekly paycheck that you're going to rely on. You're not freelance the minute you become professional.

W: You can know that you have your expenses covered. That you have a baseline.

C: Exactly. And if you were working-class kid, the fact that you're getting a paycheck on a regular basis is super important.

W: So we talked about training as a definite advantage, but what else did the Brits know that we didn't and how did they manage to infiltrate the system here so thoroughly? We have Brits in every show playing roles in ensemble casts and as co-leads. Do you think it's because we are a worldwide global community now? Internet and access to tape everywhere?

C: That and money has a lot to do with it. Because in England they were selling their shows to England or PBS, which doesn't exactly pay big but now you have such a fractured business, that it's hard for people except big stars to make any money, right? Certainly not what the networks used to pay.

W: It's a new landscape for sure and ever changing. Let's pivot and talk about the audition room ... We are largely virtual for first auditions. We use Eco-cast, you use Spotlight. So now with those platforms and everything being virtual, are we exactly the same? Or are there major differences?

C: It's much more similar. The thing is, it used to be that people got panicked because they didn't audition that often for "on screen" stuff. It was a real mix of auditioning for stage and they felt very non-confident in their filming ability. I used to do some workshops to help with that in which I would always say: "The truth, is the truth, is the truth." It doesn't matter where the screen or stage is. It's about kinetics. Remember that theatre is a play performed for an audience. Without an audience, there is no theatre. But we also know that if you shoot a comedy, and the crew laughs it tanks when you see it on screen.

W: Why?

C: Because you're projecting to the crew. You're playing for the crew. You're including the crew as your audience but there's an innate difference because that's theatre, not film. So, it's not that the performance needs to be small or more "conversational." We've always been conversational! It's about letting the camera do the work.

W: You do need to understand the dynamics that you can use on your behalf.

C: But it doesn't have to be small. Al Pacino, De Niro, I mean all the greats ... they let the camera do the work. They're not projecting it. And they've learned that skill, whether they learn it through trial and error, or they just been naturally that way or whatever, but they understand innately the kinetics and that's what I keep telling people. I say "don't think of big performance, small performance, do not squash it . . . the truth is the truth, right? You want to be in the moment and in the character. But let the camera do the work."

W: Any more advice? You had told me something about leaning in? And the importance of stretching?

C: Yes, think about it. When you're leaning forward it feels like what you're doing is pleading. "Please give me a job" and "I'm not sure if I can really do this." I always tell them remember that the person on the other side of the table is afraid of making the wrong decision. He's afraid of being made fun of when they look at the dailies or when they look at the film, and say "who hired that actor?" So don't play into fear, which means, stand up straight and tell me "I can do the job." And, full body relaxation. No more than 10–15 minutes before you go in. Literally, pull your arms over your head, reach up and fully stretch until you can't, and then release and bend with your arms to the floor. It greatly reduces tension when you work through the body that way.

W: What do you think about actors holding sides?

C: I don't mind it at all. I'd much rather have an actor who *knows* the scene, than an actor who's *memorized* the scene because it makes it really hard for them to change and make an adjustment. If I say to them, "Listen, in the beginning of the scene, you've got to be far more nervous and you only start to calm down once you reach this part of the scene" they can't do it because they've drilled the rhythm over and over and over to memorize and it's hard to switch gears.

W: It's also hard to identify what place you're giving them that adjustment if they don't have the paper in hand to visually see the shift.

C: Well, also one of the first things I tell people, particularly young actors, is to take your sides and write them out with no stage directions and nothing that says "pause" or "laugh" or anything because you will be different than everybody else. Everybody else is going to look at the spacing of the lines on the page. And that's when the pauses come subconsciously. Because of what's happening. But you will have your own version of it.

W: Great advice. Can I pivot for two last pieces of the conversation? Are you all self-tapes right now?

C: No, we've gone back to auditions as well. Self-tapes are tough. You don't know if they've done multiple takes or only had five minutes and did something on the spot. Also, we're not sitting with the producers most of the time when they're looking at the tapes and there are ways to finesse a self-tape audition with information we may know about that actors "up-and-coming" work or give more context historically on their behalf.

W: And last, what about representation in the UK. Do you have to have an agent and be represented in the UK to get work?

C: Yes. Not necessarily the second you get out because some Rep companies will, for example, audition a lot of local actors. So they're outside of London and there's some people who don't want to leave London but the biggest difference is that the agents in the UK can tell their actors the truth.

W: Why?

C: Because if you move agents more than once or twice during your entire career, the problem is you, not your agent. In the US, people leave their agents, sometimes three or four times and nobody makes a comment. You just got to look up whoever they're with now. In the UK, they get picked up in drama school when they're babies. And by agents, we don't have managers. So agents are managers, and they tough talk them and take care of them. You know, I was just talking to somebody at a big agency they were saying "yes, when we had to get so-and-so's teeth fixed, and we set up an account for his taxes." So when he's gotten a series, he has the money to pay his taxes, etc.

W: Wow, so they really handle all the aspects of their lives.

C: Yeah. Because the thing is, they're expecting to have that actor for their entire career. That's the norm. So their relationship's deeper, and they're not so insecure.

W: A lot of consistency, a lot of solidarity, a lot of loyalty. Those are not words that you would typically attribute to Hollywood!

C: In the US it's okay to leave your agent even after they get a huge deal for you. It's okay socially to do that but in the UK, it's not.

W: I hear that. That's a huge difference in work ethics.

C: That's why English actors are around much longer. They last much longer. One is because they can go home every weekend when they're young and don't have any money and their mates will take the "mickey" out of them. If they get, you know, an overblown head. So, you have a chance of becoming and staying a normal person . . . and that is the most important thing at the end of the day. I was always taught there's always room for "please" and "thank you." In other words, be a good person.

Lisa Zambetti, CSA, Casting Director

Lisa Zambetti is an Artios nominated casting director for TV, film, commercials, and video games (*Criminal Minds, Beyond Borders, Reservation Dogs*). She was recently nominated as "Video Game Casting Director of the Year" by the Talent Managers Association. She's currently casting projects for Audible and Skydance. Lisa is an active member of the Equity in Entertainment committee for the Casting Society and is on the advisory board for Hire Survivors Hollywood. As an acting teacher, Lisa is on the faculty of UCLA and has also taught for USC, UC Santa Barbara, Cal State East Bay, Whitman College, and Pace University.

The world of motion capture casting

Wendy: What exactly is motion capture casting? What are the projects that fall into this category?

Lisa: In video games there is Voice Over (just the actors voice, no visual, which requires voice dexterity in texture, tone, accent, expression, volume) and Motion Capture (the actors body moving and doing actions like running, driving, flying, jumping rolling, climbing, fighting, walking, crawling, which requires movement skills and body expressivity). Some videos games go deeper and require Performance and Likeness Capture which means an actor's full facial expression as well as emotional acting skills come into play. These are full scenes that can have all kinds of emotional requirements, rage, love, longing, revenge, terror, joy, and the "cameras" are capturing all of that just like in a regular movie or TV show. However, in performance capture, while the actor's acting is shown, their real physical features might be obscured, for example they could be playing a dragon, or a creature, or a robot, or a person with other very different appearance. Likeness Capture means the character will look almost EXACTLY like the actor. You can think of it as an animation of the actor in the game.

W: Is it important to have acting skills for this medium?

L: Oh it is imperative! We must FEEL for these characters in these games. They are not just chess pieces, we have to follow their storylines, which can be extremely complex.

W: What would be the kind of training that would enhance castability in this medium?

L: Any good well-rounded theatre training program would be great for an actor who wants to do games. Many times the games have very high stakes, like Shakespeare, or Greek plays, so training to have the physical/vocal stamina as you would in a five-act play is very important.

W: In the virtual world of self-tapes, how would someone audition for a role in a motion capture project?

L: It is exactly the same, except you might be asked to show more of your body and movement in a scene. You might want to incorporate an action (make tea, sharpening a sword, crawling through a window) or walking around the space more than in a regular audition. But it depends on the material.

W: Does improvisation play a large role in this medium?

L: Sometimes yes and sometimes no, it depends on the script and the director. Sometimes a director is totally fine with playing fast and loose with the script. However in game scripts there are many "clues" and things that MUST be articulated in order for the "player" to follow, so sometimes you do need to be word perfect.

W: Are there specific criteria that must be upheld either in the script or world that the story lives in? If yes, what are they?

L: These games are shot in a massive "black box" soundstage with really no set. So an actor must really be able to concentrate and remember where things are … where was the door I just came through? Where is the wall? Where did I just jump down from? It takes immense concentration because of course at the same time, you have a camera rig on your head recording your every expression. There are certain things you learn along the way like, *never* touch your face, and your "mo cap" suit will not have pockets so if you are an actor who is always acting with your hands in your pockets or playing with your hair ... those behaviors will not work.

W: What kind of direction can an actor expect in the casting room for the CD? From the director?

L: Sometimes you will be asked in an audition to do a character "walk" (walk around like you are the character). You will sometimes be asked to give more volume to your voice (sometimes there is a vocal test to hear how loud you can shout, especially in a combat scene). You may be asked to be very subtle then the next moment very, very big.

W: Is this a good training ground for other areas of scripted content?

L: I think it will certainly strengthen your concentration and make you fearless!

W: What are the best pieces of advice for an actor just starting out in this medium? Are there opportunities to get non-union experience first?

L: I've never worked on a non-union game but I am sure there are some. When you have the opportunity to take a class with a real mo-cap director or actor, try it out. But note, if you are not already a stunt person, you should not be asked to do stunts nor should you pay a lot of money to "train" to do stunts. If you are hired as an actor, that is what is most important and someone else will be hired to do the "flywork."

Candido Cornejo, CSA, Casting Director

Candido is a proud Latinx trans casting professional with over 10 years of experience in the entertainment industry. She has worked with prestigious casting offices including veterans Ronnie Yeskel, Fern Champion, Scott Genkinger, and Pam Dixon. Prominent credits include *The Hatfields & McCoys*, the Freeform hit show *The Fosters*, and the Artios award-winning production of *Zoot Suit* for the Center Theatre Group. Candido is a strong advocate for diversity and inclusion, particularly for the Latinx and trans/nonbinary communities. As of recent, she has completed casting for *The Answer To My Prayer* executive produced by Eddie James Olmos and Nancy De Los Santos, and two films for the "Launchpad" season 2 for Disney+ where she launched a worldwide search for a 2 Spirit Teenager for the first ever of its kind shown on a major platform.

Diversity in casting and learning the language of a casting director

Wendy: When we first met I loved hearing about your former career with Loreal. How did the skills from that profession translate to what you are doing now?

Candido: It's really funny. I actually grew in Loreal as I grew in casting. I used to work behind the counter at a Macy's for Lancome while I was interning at a casting office. Once I landed my first paid casting assistant job, I left Macy's but I still freelanced for Lancome on the weekends. There was a time when it worked out really well because I could go back and forth when things got slow. When I was offered a junior executive level at Lancome, things did change. I had to do that full time. I had to step away from casting for a bit, but it really helped me as it was a very crucial time in my life. It's when I fell in love for the first time. I was able to experience the full fantasy and adventure, and then tragedy struck and I lost him. He passed away so I had to fully step away from a lot of things so I could mourn. I was able to travel the world, dare myself to dance on stage with my favorite artists, and finally step into myself as a queer trans woman, something he said he loved about me, and wanted me to show the world so bad. I was able to fully embrace my identity, and also step into the female executive shoes I honestly had no idea how. It was why I was afraid to come out as a trans woman, I didn't know it could be possible as there is often no place for us in society. And it was difficult. There were a lot of barriers I had to fight within the company, a lot of biases and old school thinking, but I also had support. I was able to educate a corporation that indeed you can have a trans woman of color as a leader for conservative brand at a corporate level. And do it in style. I was missing casting however. I was doing a few indies here and there, but I missed doing it full time. When the pandemic hit, and they got rid of our entire department at Lancome, a producer called me up and said he needed help to cast something. I knew then it was time to come back. It was at the LALIFF Film Festival in 2021 that I reappeared, this time in my heels and lipstick. I wore my beloved's red suit in fact, as I knew it meant a great deal to him as it belonged to his mother. I wanted to honor him. I was nervous and scared to death, but when my old friends greeted me and hugged me, without a care in the world, I felt such a relief. I could breath finally. I've embraced this since. I could not have done it honestly without the time I had as an executive at Lancome.

W: How and why did you choose casting as a profession?

C: I always loved movies. My Mum and Dad always watched movies as a family growing up. *Titanic* was the first movie I saw in the theatre, and I was just amazed. When I knew you could do that as a living I wanted to do nothing more. I thought I wanted to be an actor, but the more I did it the more I realized I was arguing with the director lol. My parents would bring me to LA to do acting schools in the summer, and I met a casting director by the name of Ivy Isenberg.

When I saw her work, I was like wait a minute, is this a thing? I asked her what I needed to do, and she looked at me as if I was crazy lol. But she said "watch a lot of movies and TV. Get to know your actors and directors. And maybe go to film school." And that's exactly what I did. As soon as I graduated high school I packed my bags and moved to LA and signed up for film school. During the program I met a wonderful acting coach by the name of Heidi Davis. We get along together just great. I took casting very seriously. I gained a reputation for my casting process, and so Heidi recommended me to really look into it. I graduated, got a part-time at Lancome at Macys, and began to look into internships. Heidi introduced me to Ronnie Yeskel, and the rest is history.

W: What have been some of the challenges as you navigate the business?

C: In the beginning I feel it was establishing a name for myself. I was nobody and no one wanted to take a chance. I owe *a lot* to Ronnie Yeskel, not just for taking a chance in me, but actually seeing potential in me. I worked with a lot of great people like Fern Champion, Pam Dixon, Scott Genkinger; and they all taught me so much. But I think for a long time I was very conscious of my identity. I felt different as the feminine person of color, who wanted to wear nail polish and blouse because I always felt as a woman, but people would say it was inappropriate. All my mentors and bosses were supportive, but everyone else would advise me otherwise. I remember moments when I would be at important parties or festivals, and big casting directors would laugh at me behind my back. For someone who struggles with self-identity and place in society its quite hurtful. Often I felt I wasn't taken seriously. It really took a lot of hard work to demonstrate that my work as a professional speaks for itself, not how I dress or how I identify. I worked very hard for my name to mean something. And when I came back as a full out trans woman, I made it a mission to not just defend my right of being a working professional as a trans woman, but also for others that want to and don't know how or are too afraid to do so.

W: What is the best piece of advice you were given as a rising professional?

C: Two things. Your name means everything in this business. Protect its integrity. And Pam Dixon always tells me, 'Always be nice. It's so much work to be otherwise.'

W: Tell me about the Mi Gente CSA Initiative. Why and how it was started?

C: Mi Gente has been one of *many* conversations. It's nothing new. I've been very privileged to have worked with many Latine greats like Rosalinda Morales, Pauline Ocon, Luis Valdez. And I always admired them for their tenacity in this business. I know my lived experience as a Latine person in this country. I come from immigrant parents. You're treated differently in rural America because of the color of your skin, because of the type of car your parents drive you to school in, because of what your Mom packed you for lunch. But hearing what these veterans have gone through in their professional careers was eye opening. To hear of what my predecessors have gone through was astonishing. It encouraged me to join a lot of groups that spoke on such matters and I listened. I listened for a long time. And I investigated. You can see the issues of Latine misrepresentation or the lack of in all mainstream media over the years. There are many groups of actors and working industry professionals that always talk about it, but never on such a platform. When I was appointed as a board member for CSA, and they spoke about making a possible initiative for the Latine people, I immediately volunteered, as I knew exactly what I wanted to do and say, and who to ask to join me in the conversation. It was a chance to amplify the voices of so many with the support of CSA, which has been so rewarding and eye opening.

W: Teaching emerging professionals, the casting process has been a mission of yours. Why do you feel that is an important part of the business for an actor to understand? How do you teach "casting" to someone?

C: I've had many great teachers. And I've always believed in passing the knowledge on. It deserves to. Casting is truly an art, and some of its old magic has faded over the years. I feel its important to understand its roots and its importance. Through a business stand point, why not? I know *many* people that wished they knew so many things about casting *years* ago. All the readers I've used in all the different casting offices always leave with their eyes wide and just amazed and saying, "I had no idea! Omg!" And they get to empathize with us behind the table or camera. They also get a unique understanding of all the political things that do happen behind closed doors that aren't taught to actors. It's that decision-making that often actors don't understand that I feel makes it easier in their career to comprehend, especially when people take things a bit too personally.

W: What is the best part of your job?

C: Seeing the final result. Watching your cast come together to create something amazing. Just watching an actor bring a character to life in an audition is magical. When I feel something in me awaken, when an actor can make me feel deeply, as I do when I watch a film at home like when I was a kid, that's when I love my job. The instant gratification.

W: What is the least favorite aspect of your job?

C: When people forget to be human. We all have lives. We all have issues. We all have feelings. There's no need to make others' lives tougher. Life is short. It can be snuffed out in an instant. Why not just be kind?

W: For our industry to embrace diversity mandates, there needs to be a clear understanding of the objectives to be achieved. What are some of those objectives and how would you like other professionals to educate themselves?

C: There needs to be a thorough understanding of not just ourselves, but others. There needs to be a tremendous amount of education for people to move forward, and somethings require some of us to sit in discomfort. We must be able to step outside of ourselves in order to see the bigger picture and the main objectives, and that can be difficult sometimes. What I always tell people when it comes to education on really heavy subjects is, can you handle the hard questions, and even more so, are you prepared to hear the answer? You may not be equipped right now to hear it. How can you be?

W: What are your thoughts regarding actors playing something that is not authentic to them personally but argue that they are "actors" and should be allowed to play any role they choose?

C: Actors should be able to play anything. They are actors after all. However, can we truly tiptoe around the issues with under-represented and marginalized communities? An actor saying I should get this part because I'm an actor and nothing more, and taking away an opportunity from someone that does have that lived experience, and that lived experience and representation is crucial for the survival of certain communities, is a continuation of oppression of said communities. In the end, yes, the trained actor or the more notable name may get the part anyway, but I deepen the conversation with: Well why haven't people of that community received that sort of training or education or opportunity? It's those communities that deserve a chance to not only be seen as existent in the mainstream media, but also be given an opportunity in an industry they never believed to be a career at all.

Cassandra Han, CSA, Casting Director

Cassandra's career in film, television, and theatre has spanned more than 30 years. As a casting director, she has worked on projects for Netflix, Sky, Twentieth Century Fox, ARD/Degeto, Gaumont, Barefoot Films, Wildside, Letterbox, Lieblingsfilm, Big Window, and Cattleya; and for illustrious directors such as Terrence Malick, James Mangold, Giuseppe Tornatore, Dror Zahavi, Til Schweiger, and Stefan Ruzowitsky. New York film and television production credits include Jim Carroll's *The Basketball Diaries* with Mark Wahlberg and Leonardo DiCaprio and the PBS documentary series "The Human Language." Cassandra has also worked extensively as a writer, editor, dramaturg, and translator, specializing in adapting German and Italian screenplays and pitch materials into English. In her early career, she worked for Broadway producer Richard Frankel, as well as at the Tony Award-winning La Jolla Playhouse and Opera Company of Philadelphia. Cassandra co-founded and helped run two New York theatre companies, including Ethan Hawke's Malaparte. Cassandra holds a Master of Fine Arts from Trinity Repertory Conservatory and a Bachelor of Arts from the University of Pennsylvania. She is a founding member of Women in Film, Television and Media Italia and a member of the Casting Society (CSA) and the International Casting Directors Network (ICDN). She was a jury member for the 2021 European *Shooting Stars* and a voter for the International Emmy Awards.

Casting perspective from Central Europe

Wendy: Tell me a little about your journey into casting and what kind of projects you predominantly work on.

Cassandra: I sort of fell into casting back in the early 90s, when I worked for a Broadway producer on a show that had a number of tours. After that, I did background on a feature film that Sheila Jaffe and Georgianne Walken were casting and they sort of took me under their wing. I eventually started doing my own projects, and then it was off to the races – until I moved to Europe in 2003. It took me about a decade to figure out that I could also cast in Europe, and now I actually work much more than I did in New York. I found a really interesting niche, which is all about crossing markets. A lot of American producers, for example, have a hard time navigating the European landscape – and European producers also find it difficult to work smoothly with American or British agents. My main markets are Italy and Germany, due to language and knowledge of the talent pool.

W: How often are you tasked with collaborating on a project with a casting director from the US for European/American co-productions?

C: I very often bring the Italian or German piece to an American production, but those aren't actually co-productions, usually, due to differences in funding models and legal issues. American productions normally hire a European service producer, and that's a bit of a different relationship. But I work on European co-productions very often; most European productions require more than one country in order to raise enough money to cover the budget.

W: What advice would you give American actors looking to work in Germany or Europe?

C: To be honest, the vast majority of European productions won't hire American actors who are based in the US because going union is too expensive and the process of signing a GR1 tends to be a bit intimidating. I see this as a real shame, because American actors are sort of automatically removed from that market—usually we replace them with UK actors. If a SAG-AFTRA actor lives in Europe, it's no problem . . . so I guess I'd say "Move to Europe"!

W: How does an American actor go about getting on your radar screen?

C: I only really hire American actors who are bankable enough to attract world sales onto projects. I do a lot of development casting, actually, but in that case I am only interested in actors whose name value cancels out the extra costs related to the GR1.

W: We have BFA and MFA programs in the US. Where do actors get their training in Germany and Central Europe?

C: There are a number of very high-level conservatories in Europe, and the training is very similar to a BFA or MFA program. One difference in most European countries is that you have to pass a state exam to graduate, which is kind of like possessing a "license to act" if you will. Of course we can still cast actors who don't have that formal state approval, but having it is a big deal.

W: What do you appreciate in a self-tape? Clean background vs some "production" value.

C: I definitely appreciate it when there's nothing distracting in the background. But I also feel like the atmosphere of a background can help transport me into the world of the character—and it also helps the other decision-makers who perhaps aren't as accustomed to extrapolating as we casting directors are. For example, one actor that we cast as a Roman governor in *Barbarians* for Netflix taped against a backdrop of a wood-paneled wall. And that didn't distract the viewer, but conveyed so much in a very simple way: wealth, education, power, sophistication.

W: What is the best overall advice you can give to actors looking to enter the business?

C: It's a marathon, not a sprint. Don't expect things to happen quickly, and you have to be in it for the long-haul.

W: What methods do you employ to learn new actors and source talent for auditions?

C: Mostly platforms, although I also attend the theatre and watch a lot of shows.

W: How often will your guidance and relationship with the talent change the casting outcome?

C: I am very honest with actors, and often have them re-tape if I think that they have a good shot but somehow that's not visible on screen. It's happened many times that the actor I asked to re-tape with a different direction gets the job in the end.

W: How do you like talent to stay in touch with you?

C: Only email, and please don't be hurt if I don't answer. I always categorize emailed pitches and I do source actors from there quite often. Unsolicited calls or texts are really invasive, and I generally don't recommend that actors DM casting directors on social media either.

Nikki Barrett, CSA, CGA, Casting Director, Barrett Casting/Australia

Nikki Barrett has been casting Australian and international film and television for over 20 years. Her work includes acclaimed features such as *Elvis, Thirteen Lives, The Power of the Dog, Ticket to Paradise, Mad Max: Fury Road, The Babadook, Nitram, Hacksaw Ridge, I Am Mother, Peter Rabbit, The Proposition, Maos Last Dancer, The Sapphires, Somersault, The Railway Man,* and *Candy.* Television work includes the upcoming series, "Boy Swallows Universe," "Bay Of Fires" and "Black Snow."

Meet Nikki Barrett!

Wendy: How is the Australian market similar/different from the American market and how does the audition process differ from practices in the US?

Nikki: I feel like the experience is probably very similar but smaller. As Australians come out, they're conquering the local market, but they're also focused on how to come to America. But it's different for different people. I think what everyone's always looking for is to have the most options within their career. Some people come out very focused on England, a lot of young people come out and are very focused on America and then some want to stay here and work. So, it's all the above. There was a period pre-Covid where I feel like when I used to go and talk to drama schools, they'd just be asking me questions about O-1 Visas to get to America. I think it was following Dacre Montgomery. He was cast in *Power Rangers* while still at drama school and some people thought, "well, if I can do that, I'm off." But I think that's changed a little bit post-Covid. I think people are staying here, trying to get a career, tape for things before looking overseas. That's also the advice they're now getting from American agents. There used to be this sense of "graduate, get over there, sit over there" but because people are self-taping, I think it's a much bigger sense of stay where you are, build a career, develop as an actor, tape the stuff over here and then when it happens, it happens.

W: So is your audition process similar to ours? Predominantly self-taping right now?

N: It is similar to yours and to some extent it's dictated by who you're working with and it's changing all the time. A lot of first round auditioning is now self-taping. And that's partly something that's driven by the actors' geography, because I think self-taping has allowed actors to live where they want as opposed to having to live in Sydney or Melbourne. And Sydney is prohibitively expensive to live in. So, for an actor to be able to live outside Sydney now, for example in Perth or Queensland, it's very liberating. In the last year, there's a lot of work that hasn't shot in Sydney. They've shot in Queensland or they've shot in South Australia, so I am getting a lot of tapes coming in because they're not shooting here. We're seeing a lot of interesting people from different places. Recalls, or callbacks, are mostly in the room. We've done a lot of workshops in the last two years on projects as well. I've been on projects where we've been looking for kids or we've been looking for specific areas of diversity so we're often looking in community rather than actors. And so we've done a lot of workshop situations.

W: I think we define "workshop" differently. In the US when we say "workshop" it means going out into the community and holding a workshop with a teaching objective. Is that what you mean?

N: No, for instance, we did a television series last year that was very based around the Australian South Sea Islander community, and that community is not highly represented in the acting community. So we did a big search through the community through taping originally, because that's the beauty of social media reach, and then Natalie Wall, the other casting director, did an enormous amount of Zoom auditions with people because a lot of people are up in Queensland, Far North Queensland, etc. Once we got to a shortlist, we went into workshops where we'd bring 10 people in a day and spend the whole day doing workshops, and doing improv and doing exercises. It was specific. It was a cool "callback" process.

W: Is there anything else that would surprise me about your process in Australia or the way you work that would be different than the way we work in the US in terms of releasing breakdowns, fielding actors through submissions, etc.? Is there anything unique to your marketplace that you don't see us doing here?

N: I think the world generally works fairly similarly. Obviously, it's just on a smaller scale here. It's slightly more intimate here, you know, relationships with agents, and such. We work a lot with people overseas and other countries but we can't just bring people into the country without some sort of justification and it's usually around funding or cultural specificity. For example, we did actually reach out to American agents when we were looking for a young girl and got a lot of tapes. But it was for a lead. We don't do a whole lot of support roles out of America. It tends to be people at a certain level, or sometimes very specifically, we might need. For example, I was working on something and we needed black actors from America, so I was talking to agents and asking for suggestions. I know people at a certain level, then there's a whole level of working actors that I'm not as familiar with. So occasionally when something is culturally specific to the US we reach out, but most of the time if we bring someone from the US it's a profile name.

W: How often do you collaborate with American casting directors? Did you have any specific mentors?

N:I don't do much collaboration anymore. Ronna Kress was the person that gave me entry into the whole US system. She personally connected me with Warner Brothers. We did pilots and American films together. She was a huge mentor to me and I'm very grateful. I love working in collaboration. It just doesn't happen super much because obviously through self-taping, American casting directors are easily able to test actors themselves.

W: When talent is not represented how much interface do you have when you're casting a project with unrepresented actors?

N: Well, obviously, the problem lies in not knowing about them. If an unrepresented actor came up, and seemed good for us, we would take it from there. Or if we found actors through some kind of community search that aren't represented, obviously that's fine. The biggest problem generally for people who don't have representation is how will you know about them.

W: We have a school system with BFA/MFA programs where many artists emerge out of those programs. Do you have that?

N:Yes, we basically have four top public schools. We have institutes like NIDA (National Institute of Dramatic Art, University of New South Wales) where people like Mel Gibson, Cate Blanchette, Judy Davis, Richard Roxburgh, and Hugo Weaving came from. It's produced an amazing body of people. We also have WAAPA(University of Western Australia) which is where Hugh Jackman and Dacre Montgomery graduated, then there's QUT in Queensland and there's VCA in Victoria. So, there are four that are really quite famous, the four big conservatory schools. Then there's a lot of other schools that are reputable and good and there's some private schools like The Actors Centre. So I think school is quite a normal pathway here, but definitely not the only pathway.

W: I'm curious … because when I was talking to Carol Dudley, one of the things that was striking to me about London was that when these actors do go through university training, the matriculation into regional companies is immediate. They train and then get immediate experience to become working actors. The system supports that. Do you have something similar to that?

N:There used to be a pathway going back to Jim Sharman (*Rocky Horror*) who was one of the artistic directors of the South Australian Theatre Company, along with a number of other amazing theatre directors. They did provide a pathway for graduates into a one to two year contract but so did Sydney and Melbourne theatre companies. This still happens to some extent but is less entrenched than it was going back 20 years.

The big theatre companies do absorb a lot of new graduates, but it's not quite as established or guaranteed as the British system, and it's probably because the British system has so much theatre, repertory, and local theatre which was where, you know, there's an amazing company called Bell Shakespeare that takes a lot of new graduates and they do a lot of big mainstage stuff and then they take them which was where, you know, they take them on a massive six month tour through regional towns, which is an incredible experience for young graduates to have. But they're pretty unique in that sense.

There is also the Sydney Theatre Company, Belvoir Street, other big state theatre companies and little theatre companies. There's quite a lot of independents and companies that also use students. It's not a guaranteed pathway, but it's certainly not an uncommon one.

W: Let's talk further about being an emerging artist in your marketplace. What are some of the pitfalls or challenges that you see emerging actors falling into? What advice would you give to somebody emerging? For instance, the actor who is just having a chance for the first time to come in and interface with your office?

N: What used to be really great is when pilot season existed, graduates would come out November/December and pilot season started in January. We used to use them as readers all the time. And so they'd be in the room and we get to know them and they'd get to just work day after day. It was fantastic. But "pilot season" has kind of disappeared, we don't have it as much anymore. Which is unfortunate because it was a really good way to learn new talent. As for advice, here is what I often say to students:

1 Understand what is uniquely yours, and don't try and fit into some mold or be a generic version of what you think will fit somewhere. I think what people forget is that the people who succeed out in the world are people who are quite distinct. You know, like Tilda Swinton is very distinct. Sam Rockwell was very distinct. You know, even someone who's classically beautiful like Cate Blanchet is still very distinct. She knows who she is and it's something to understand what you have that's uniquely yours and utilize that to find some way to make a mark, rather than trying to make up some generic version of what you think is going to succeed in the world. Understand and value what's uniquely yours.

2 Make choices about your career, and you can change them. For example: my focus is, I want to work in theatre for the next two years and therefore I should be looking across theatre companies, and what they're doing and I should be understanding texts and across my accent. Or, I want to go to England and work on the BBC and comedy, so I need to get on top of my accents and British programming/rhythms. If you come up through these highly structured environments, where you go to school for years, and you're told what to do, every moment of the day is filled, and then suddenly you're spat out in the world, and there's just nothing, you know? So, build some structure for yourself where you can still wake up every day being an actor, have purpose, and feel like you're doing something for your career. Even if you're not getting employed, you're moving forward in some way. If you're not getting work, try and create work with friends, transform everything. I mean, really practical stuff.

3 Move at your own pace. I always say to students that everybody moves at a different pace. It's really hard when you come out of a group of 20 people, and the next week someone may sign up for the lead and someone may go to America and get a job and someone may be in a theatre company, and some may not even have an agent. I always think give it five years, you know, everyone finds their place in the world at different speeds. And, don't panic about that. I know that's really hard, but just try to keep focused on your path and not to worry too much about what's happening with everyone else.

W: I love what you're saying so much, because it's as if you're writing a chapter of the book! It always gives me a lot of pleasure to hear that other colleagues share the same philosophy and encouragement.

N: It's about empowering yourself and not feeling disempowered, so everybody is at the mercy of what's being made. Do anything you can to empower yourself, to expand as an actor and a human being and go out and experience life and do all those things that just are going to make you better and more interesting.

Marci Liroff, Casting Director/Intimacy Coordinator

From her decades of experience in audition rooms as a casting director and on set as a producer and acting coach, Liroff has seen first-hand how this industry can treat actors. With the #MeToo movement and #TimesUp movement, Intimacy Coordination has been created to ensure that the actors, filmmakers, and crew are kept informed, educated, and safe during scenes of intimacy and nudity. Her years of work in film and television production, along with her communication skills and keen eye, make Liroff a perfect in the world of Intimacy Coordination. She has completed an extensive training course with the premier Intimacy Coordinator, Amanda Blumenthal of Intimacy Professionals Association (IPA) and is a Certified Intimacy Coordinator. She worked on Season: 2 and 3 of the series "Hightown" for STARZ, "BOSCH: LEGACY," "General Hospital," and the limited series "SUGAR" for HBO for Apple TV. For more information on Marci, visit www.marciliroffIC.com.

An intimate conversation about intimacy on set

Wendy: Take us through the job of an intimacy coordinator. What are the main ingredients of the job?

Marci: The intimacy coordinator, or IC, collaborates with the actors and the filmmaking team to ensure that scenes of intimacy (simulated sex and/or nudity, kissing) are done with authenticity and safety. We're like a stunt coordinator for intimate scenes.

W: Can you walk through who you work most closely with on set? How does the conversation differ between the various creatives, i.e. the director, 1st AD?

M: I work closely with several department heads, but mostly I work with the performers and the director. I also work with Hair and Makeup to make sure that they are aware of what is called for in the scene. Makeup can apply artificial sweat, Hair needs to make sure that there's continuity between scenes.

I work with the wardrobe department to let them know what the scene entails. For instance, if a couple is jumping in bed and simulating sex, if the female actor is wearing tights it would add another step to the scene that perhaps we don't want. The wardrobe department often supplies the modesty garments that we use. The FCC and SAG/AFTRA have rules against actual genital on genital action. There must be a modesty garment and sometimes padding between the performers.

I first talk to the director to find out how they see the scene in a creative sense. We want to make sure we're telling their story in an authentic way. Is the scene meant to be hot and sexy? Tender and loving? Every movement tells the story. Sometimes the director has very specific ideas and sometimes they have me do all the choreography. We note which body parts will be shown in a very specific way. Then I talk to each actor in a private one-on-one meeting to discuss these ideas, see what their ideas are, discuss consent and boundaries, and determine whether I'm hearing what we call "enthusiastic consent" from the actor. If they have any hesitation, I hear them out and we find a workaround and I check with the director to see if they're on board and if we're all on the same page. Then I work with the legal department to help them draft the nudity rider for said scene. There's a rider for each scene.

I work with the AD department to have them assure a closed set for the scene. A closed set means only essential personnel are allowed to be on set or view the monitor. Since many sets have several monitors all over the set, we flag or tent these monitors so they're not open for all to view. The PAs assure this security. On the day, I'm usually going back and forth between the monitor and the set to check-in on the actors and confer with the director.

I'm also trained in trauma first aid. Sometimes a performer can be triggered by something within the scene and I am trained to see if they're having any issues and help them through it. I can also help the crew if they're having any issues. Imagine we're shooting a violent simulated sex scene and the crew is watching it over and over. They can get triggered too.

I'm also an advocate for the LGBTQIA+ community. A lot of my job is providing education for the crew. For instance, I had a wardrobe supervisor who refused to use the correct pronouns for a trans performer.

W: Do you have the ability to say, "cut" if you see unauthorized exposure or something the actor has expressed concern over? Or, do you wait till the scene is over and then flag the problem?

M: The only people calling "cut" on a set are the director or the ADs. If something goes sideways during a scene, I will go to the AD to ask them to pause until we sort it out. If I see a body part exposed that is not cleared on the nudity rider I flag it with the script supervisor so that it cannot be used in the final cut.

W: Are you ever asked to be present during the audition process?

M: So far I have not. BUT, the ICs have a committee that worked closely with SAG/AFTRA to add new clauses to the 2020 contract which protects them in an audition situation and on set.

W: How much prep/conversation do you have with the actors before they shoot the scene?

M: A large portion of my work is prep. I have very in-depth conversations with the performers before the shooting day to plan out *exactly* what the scene will be—sometimes we have rehearsal time set aside. These conversations can be similar to an intake interview that a therapist would have with a new client. I like to know if they have any injuries we should be concerned with. For instance, if they have a bad knee, I will avoid putting them on their knees. If they're concerned about showing their stomach, then I'll be conscientious about using a bed sheet to cover them if possible. I'm watching on the monitor to make sure that body parts don't show that they haven't agreed to and also to make sure that the angle they're being shot is attractive if that's what the storyline is. Sometimes the scene is meant to be rough and messy and we're not concerned with "beauty" per se.

W: What have been some of the unexpected challenges you've encountered in your work?

M: Unfortunately, since this job is still in its infancy there are directors, producers, actors, and crew who are not fully educated on the width and breadth of this position and what we can offer and what we're responsible for. There can be an inherent pushback to anything new. I find that those that aren't confident in their skills aren't great at collaboration.

W: How did your training as a casting director help you with this line of work?

M: A large part of the job is "playing well with others." Since I've worked as a casting director, producer and acting coach for 40+ years, I have this experience in spades. Having actual on set experience is crucial to this job and can't be taught. Because of my work as an acting coach and teacher, I can help the actor during their intimate scenes in a more specific way. Because there is so much prep before the actual shooting day, the actor knows exactly what to expect on the day and there are no surprises.

W: Who advocates for an emerging actor (who may not have a team of management or representation) if there is an issue or problem?

M: That's exactly why I'm there throughout the whole process to advocate for actors.

Writer/Producer

Jonathan Prince, Writer/Producer/President PhilmCo Media

Jonathan Prince, is a prolific writer/producer/showrunner with a passion for stories driven by character ... and often accompanied by a noteworthy soundtrack. His journey from Harvard to Hollywood has been marked with work as an actor (starring in two television series), director (television series, pilots, and feature films), and writer/producer (over 275 hours of programming). He's worked with legendary stars like Mary Tyler Moore, Gene Wilder, Whoopi Goldberg, and Mick Fleetwood, partnering with producers like Jimmy Iovine, Mindy Kaling, Robert Redford, Dick Clark, and Billy Porter to create shows for Amazon, Hulu, HBO, Disney, Apple, Netflix, and multiple cable and broadcast networks.

Importance of creating original material

Wendy: How did your training as an actor inform your career as a writer/producer?

Jonathan: I never formally trained as an actor. My "training" was my work growing up in high school, acting in high school shows as well as a summer repertory company and doing college theatre as an actor. So the training that I got was from the directors who directed me and working on the words that were written for me—which gave me great respect for words and direction. My "training" such as it is, taught me how to listen to how people speak. Not just how they speak to each other in scripted dialogue, but how they speak in terms of a director instructing an actor in prose. From "Stand over there, Pick up this glass" to the more nuanced direction of emotion, motivation, and all that goes into helping me, as an actor, create a performance. And in writing, as an actor, I paid attention to the stage directions given by the writer. For example, the parenthetical intention that accompanies the dialogue—the adverb that goes with the dialogue. When I write, I write with voices in my head. The voices of the director, the voices of the writer—the voices of the actors I was blessed to work with. You know, the writer works in a strange medium. We write our script on paper or on a computer screen, but it's never intended to be digested that way by the audience. This isn't a novel. In fact, these scripts—whether for stage or screen—are intended to be listened to, or watched. So ... with that in mind, and thinking about my training—I think I had an advantage because I grew up thinking a lot about how things sounded versus just how they read on the page.

W: How were you able to make the transition from actor to writer/producer?

J: I was very lucky. And also ambitious. I was on a television series as an actor. I had been a stage actor for many years and when I left law school I decided to pursue a career as a full-time actor. I was lucky enough to get "discovered" doing an Equity waiver musical in Los Angeles. That musical, the West Coast premiere of the Elizabeth Swados show *Runaways*, got me an agent and although I was 21 or 22 years old, I looked very young for my age, so I was cast to play a 16-year-old (not uncommon in those days on a television show) in a half-hour, scripted, filmed show. So it wasn't a sitcom. We weren't on stage all the time. It was shot more like a one-hour drama or a movie. Which meant that I had a lot of free time. And my mentors on the set were actors like Barnard Hughes, who played the lead of that show, and great directors like Bill Bixby, John Astin, Leo Penn, Howie Storm, and Harry Winer. I found when I wasn't listening to the director, or working with the other actors rehearsing or shooting, I was bored. I had been used to the intellectual sort of excitement of being either on a college campus, or the full-time attention demanded by the theatre. The other actors, when they weren't working, were in their trailers, reading the paper or having a smoke, even reading other scripts. So I went into the writers' room and I talked to the Executive Producers—Larry Rosen and Larry Tucker—incredibly talented guys who ran the writers and said, "You know, when I have free time on the set, do you mind if I come and sit in the writers' room and listen?" And they said, "Why, because you want to write yourself a bigger part?" I said, "No, a smaller part . . . I'd like to learn to write for TV." And they said, "What makes you think you could be a writer?" to which I replied: "I dunno— Harvard English major so I figure I can write something. I just have to learn the format." (This is before Final Draft and the ease with which a newcomer can learn the formatting. Back then, it was all a mystery.) And so, thanks to "the Larry's" I sat in the room. I listened a lot, learned a lot and read a lot. And then I wrote a spec episode of that show I was on and that started my writing career.

W: What do young creatives need to know when they're trying to develop their own materials?

J: I think there's two reasons for young creatives to develop their own material. One is if you are a young performer, and you're looking to create material that will show you off as an actor. That's one type of material. It's very specific. That is to say, it only has to be good for you. It only has to show you off, whether it's a monologue, scene, play, or even a pilot. And that comes with a warning label, which is: What if you're not the right person to play the part? So be prepared that, in success, you'll give it up. (NOTE: But that would mean you're successful!) The other reason to write something if you're a young creative, is—as I always say to every actor—"What's the thing you're doing when you're not acting? What's the thing that keeps you excited and interested? The thing you can't wait to get back to so that although you're in an audition and it feels like the stakes are high, you actually have this other project that's calling your name and you can't wait to get back to write." That play, scene, monologue, pilot, spec feature—that is the thing you're writing for two reasons. One is because you like it and you think you've got a story to tell, but also, because you'd like to see yourself as a writer and you don't see yourself in it. You are not writing a part for yourself. You're writing it because you think it's good writing or a great story to be told or you could sell it. So those are the two ways I would look at it.

W: What are the tools that an actor or writer need to help sell a project?

J: Wouldn't it be great if all projects were sold on their own merit? That is to say, not judged by who wrote it, and not who has told the story out loud in the pitch, but just by what's on the paper? I said in an earlier question that scripts are meant to be heard, but unfortunately, that's not how they're bought. They're bought by somebody reading it and a piece of paper doesn't speak for itself. Too often, a buyer will say, "Who wrote this?" They want to know before they read it. To use art as an analogy, if they know Picasso painted the piece, they would be more inclined to like it. We judge a painting that we love, by the painter, and sometimes not by the painting itself. "Oh, it's by Picasso, therefore, I am more inclined to like it" versus "Oh, it's by some unknown artist, I guess it may not be that good." And this extends beyond the script that's read. There's further advantage that come to the actor/writer when it comes to verbally pitching a story. When an actor pitches a story, it's entertaining, it's exciting, whereas a writer may not be comfortable with pitching. Which puts them at a distinct disadvantage, because at that moment in time, it's not about the writing. It's about the telling of the story out loud. So, I think the things that I would say to writers is—you can't fix the first: you can't suddenly become Picasso. Unless you are! So, instead, focus on the second. Which is be the someone who can tell this story out loud in a room, at a cafe or a diner. Think of it as a performance piece. Which means it has to have a shape to it that is pointedly about entertaining. First, bring your audience (your buyer) in with one incredibly entertaining part of the story in the beginning. Get them leaning forward. Then, tell the story quickly, let them know that they're in the hands of a master. "I am taking you on a journey. I know exactly where I'm going. Here's the GPS: I'm going to tell you about the characters, the pilot story, the rest of the season and then move forward." And then bring them in with a great closing. Because you're goal is not only or specifically to sell your show or film or play—it's to sell yourself so that the next time you're selling, you may not be Picasso, but you're not totally unknown. They remember you from this first pitch. You're memorable. And that means memorable from the beginning and memorable at the end. You don't take too long in the middle. I always say that pitches are like a first date. You have to get them to like you. Get them to delight in the experience of listening to you and wanting to hear from you again because you're not really just pitching your project. You're pitching yourself.

W: This is a little bit more of a lengthy question. I'm looking for a kind of play by numbers, or Greatest Hits answer to: what is the trajectory from that pitch meeting into development and then eventually production? Take me on a brief journey once I've sold the idea in the room. What next?

J: And are we talking film or television because they're slightly different? Let's talk about television first. The trajectory really begins with what did you sell them? Did you sell them the idea and the treatment? Because then it needs to go to script. Did you sell them a script? Because then it needs to be rewritten (since inevitably, everything needs to be rewritten). But the general trajectory would be you've sold them something that's specific enough that there will be a development phase in which the idea becomes a script. And then the script becomes a better script. And that's how that pilot episode for that pilot and series idea that you pitched gets to the next place. It goes from producer or production company to a studio, or from producer or production company directly to the buyer like Disney +, AMC, or Netflix. Do they choose to develop it further? That is to say, to order the pilot this year? For a first-time writer or an early-in-career writer, it would be very rare for someone to say "Great idea. Now we'll pay you lots of money to write it." And even if you've written something terrific, it would be more likely that they would assign that young writer some sort of mentor or Executive Producer to oversee the next step. TV is tough—because it's about long-term strategy and success. Multiple episodes over time. Strangely enough, in a weird way it's easier for a first-time writer to score with a feature, because a TV pilot needs to be the blueprint for lots of money being spent over—hopefully—many years of doing a television series. We did nearly 70 hours of *American Dreams* for NBC. And they had to believe that was a possibility based on a single pitch. Then a single script. Then a single pilot episode. So the blueprint has to be at the foundation firm enough and detailed enough that one might construct a building on it. Or bigger, like the *Law & Order*'s or the *CSI*'s or the current world of *Yellowstone*, not just a building but an entire eco-system. A movie is different. It's a one shot. I mean, it might become a sequel, but that's not the intention. So if you write a high-concept horror film, genre film, comedy film, thriller—whatever it is—it's super high concept and original and if the script exists, then the trajectory is different from that of televison. Your producer, production company, studio, or buyer all have the same planned trajectory, which is "We love this, we're going to option it." An option usually means they'll pay you a little money upfront for 6 months, 12 months, 18 months, during which time they'll develop it. And during that time, either they'll have you, the writer, do a rewrite or they'll bring on another writer (or writers) to do the rewrite and take it to the point at which it gets shot. An option payment which often happens with television as well is also very little money. A "shopping agreement" is another term of art. Either way—it's a little money for that first 6, 12, 18 months, and then, in success, there's always a second option. That is to say, after a year it's not ready to go but they still love it. They'll renew the option for a little more money this time with an eye on something called a "purchase price" (if they choose to move forward and make the film or the TV pilot). For example: "We paid you $1,500.00, and now we're going to pay you much more"—there's a purchase price involved for the purchase of the script or the pilot. And even as I say it, I shrug and say, "If only it were that simple. . . ." It ain't.

W: If this is something that I am self producing/developing, and not studio based, but based on my own trajectory of development, how would I get something like that into the marketplace?

J: Let's use a short film, as an example. It's 15–20 minutes long, with a beginning, middle, and end; maybe it's a documentary, maybe it's a narrative film. The thing about a short, there are portals for so many festivals that one can enter, in which there's an entry fee for a relatively small cost. You know, entering a short doc or a short film into festivals is a great idea because it gets attention. It's in the marketplace. And there are always people looking at those festivals to find people who have been awarded prizes. Festivals award numerous prizes to worthy entrants. And festivals are in the business of bringing unknown artists together to share their work with those who want to meet them and know them. It's sort of a matchmaking service. Producers, studios, and other buyers are in the business of trying to find that person who's written, produced, or directed a noteworthy short film or documentary. So I would say it's a good strategy to shoot your own short film. It's a bad strategy to shoot your own pilot because that will almost never work. If the idea is either a documentary or feature, do it as a short form, go the festival circuit. That's the way to get into those portals. If it's a full-length script or self-produced feature or pilot, it's much more difficult . . . unless you know somebody. When you are connected. To anyone in the food chain—agents, creative executives at production companies, studios, streamers, networks, cables. Connections are such a head start. So get connected. And if you can't get connected, go the festival route—and then get connected.

W: So you've lately been working with actors who are developing their own projects. Do you see a different mindset or approach from that population versus those that are coming up as strictly writers?

J: I do. I've been lucky enough to develop with emerging actors through my association with Wendy at Pace University. Many of the actors are thinking about things in which they might star and I try my darndest to commit them to something else. Many of them want to use this as something that might get people to pay attention to them as performers. What I've tried to say to them is: "You are indeed using this pitch, this project, to get people to pay attention to you . . . just remember it may not necessarily be a piece to act in and it might be that this is your time as a storyteller. Make sure that your project is not so narrow and specific that it's only for you to star in. If you're an actor, please see the merit in creating something that is *both*—from you and for you." Actors can see the merit in both. Writers never have to think that way because they're not performers. They're not coming from that space. It's only from them and never about them.

W: What are some of your "must reads" for aspiring creatives?

J: The first must-read if you're an aspiring creative, is *Letters to a Young Poet* by Rainer Maria Rilke. It's very short. You can read it in an hour. It's the most inspirational writing of a mentor/poet sending letters to this young aspiring artist, who wrote him saying: "What about romance?" "What about life?" "What about sex?" "Who am I?" And it's these wonderful letters. All real. This is all real. It took place in real time, from 1903 – 1908, real advice letters from a real master (Rilke) to a real novice (the "Young Poet"). The letters have lasted forever. It's a must-read. Must. Am I clear? Did I say "must"? Okay. In terms of, if you want to be a writer for television, just read Charles Dickens. There's no finer television writer than Charles Dickens. Every week, he had to turn out another chapter—another episode—in his story about an ongoing character: Oliver Twist, Pip, Nicholas Nickleby, Little Nell from *The Old Curiosity Shop*, or David Copperfield. He had to create their stories, week by week, just like we do in television, and keep his audience excited enough, with cliffhangers, so that they would have to buy the newspaper that week to see what happened to that character. Like any great serialized television drama. So if you want to learn about how to write serialized television with memorable characters and evocative twists and turns, take a lesson from Charles Dickens.

W: What's the material that compels you personally, that keeps you engaged?

J: I love a strongly voiced short story. That's compelling, because you can tell from the voice in the short story whether the person's got the gift to tell a story or got a craft and it doesn't involve a spec novel. Which demands a lot from the reader. I don't love reading spec features. That's not my favorite thing. I like reading spec pilots, even though I think it's a very tough game to win if you're looking to get produced. But with that, you can win admiration, or mentorship, because the beauty of a pilot, a spec pilot, is it says "I have a mindset and a gift and the craft with which I can tell stories that lasts a long time. But here's the one that will grab you." That said, I love anybody who's thinking out of the box. I don't mind reading, you know, a scene between two people, a short play. And, of course, because of my own passions, if it's intended for the theatre, I will read it. Because as a stage play, it can't use the tricks of cameras and special effects and car crashes and aliens. It's just great dialogue or great drama. So anything written for the stage, a one-act play a short play or a full-length play. That gets my attention as well.

W: If you made a movie or a TV series of your life, what genre would it be under? How would you label it? Sell it?

J: My own life? I would say it is a family drama. Both about the family I was born into and the family that I created. And even the family I wish I had created. Yeah, a family drama. But there are lots of those that are pretty darn good . . . so I'm reluctant to try. And yet, as I think about it, all of the characters I've created over my career as a writer are parts of those families—the one I was born into, the one I created, and the one I wanted. So yeah—maybe I've been writing that all along.

Mindset and study of craft

Ben Whitehair, Actor, Entrepreneur, Coach

Ben Whitehair is a champion for social change through art and business. He is a working actor in Los Angeles, and co-founded the premier online business academy and coaching community for actors, https://working. actor (https://working.actor/). Ben currently serves as the Executive Vice President of SAG-AFTRA, and is the COO of TSMA Consulting— entertainment's premier social media management and growth firm. He is a serial entrepreneur, certified business/mindset coach, and former cowboy. Ben also co-created and taught UCLA's graduate level class on social media and the business of showbiz. More info at BenWhitehair.com (http:// benwhitehair.com/), or on socials @BenWhitehair.

I'm an actor: Now what?!

"I'm an actor. It's 9am on a random Tuesday. What the hell do I *do* today to move my career forward?" This question haunted me when I first moved to Los Angeles. Ultimately, in my journey to answer that question I learned five invaluable lessons:

1 Mindset matters as much—if not more—than action steps.
2 Success looks different for everyone.
3 You must have a game plan.
4 One small step every day adds up.
5 Enjoy the journey.

I moved to LA from Colorado over a decade ago to pursue an acting career. Looking back, it's safe to say that I knew pretty much nothing about how to do that. I quickly learned that there are myriad paths in entertainment, and absolutely no set way to make a career in the arts happen. At the start all I wanted were action steps. Someone please just tell me what to do and I'll do it! Eventually I did figure out how to move forward, but it wasn't until I transformed my mindset that the actions became effective.

Lesson 1: Mindset matters as much—if not more— than action steps

I felt so annoyed when I moved to la la land that everywhere I looked the advice for actors was centered around mindset. A decade later, I get it.

The thing is, an acting career—just like any other—is a long-term pursuit. The odds of getting an agent and booking a pilot in the first six months of moving to the big city are tantamount to winning the lottery. Sure, there are lottery winners, but you are drastically more likely to have a million dollars by saving small amounts over time than by hitting the jackpot.

Similarly, adopting a long-term mindset that sets you up for happiness and abundance on a daily basis is much more likely to lead to that ultimate acting goal than simply giving it six months on hope and a prayer.

Additionally, a mindset of vision, commitment, and determination are what will have you actually execute on those action steps repeatedly over time.

Lesson 2: Success looks different for everyone

There are so many different careers as an actor. In order to determine what steps to take, you first get to decide where you want to go. Defining what success looks like—for YOU—will make the difference between happiness and struggle.

Having the courage to be honest with yourself is imperative. I hear so many actors who say that they "just want to act," but in diving deeper I find this is often disingenuous. Consider this: would you be happy if you never got paid a cent for acting for the rest of your life? Would you still say you "just want to act"? If you truly only care about performing, that's amazing. But be honest with yourself either way.

Specificity, too, is crucial. Actors often say "I just want to make a living as an actor." But again, what does that actually mean? Get specific. How much money is that (remembering to factor in agent/manager commissions, taxes, headshots, etc.)? And, if I said that you would make that amount of money but only by doing industrial commercials for your entire career would you still be ok with "just making a living as an actor"? If so, GREAT! If not, get more specific—and honest—about what your goals truly are.

Remember that this is your life. Not your friends'. Not your acting teacher's. Not your parents'. What do you want? Beyond that, how do you want to feel? What kind of lifestyle do you want? What's the impact you want to have? How do you want to spend your time on that random Tuesday? And however you define success for yourself, is the path it will take to get there in alignment with the life you imagine for yourself?

Lastly, it's more than ok if you're unclear about the answers to these questions right now. There are no right or wrong goals to have, and it may take exploring many different options; and 1, 2, or 15 years into your career your vision or mission may change. That's perfectly alright.

Lesson 3: You must have a game plan

Whether you're still exploring or dead set on a specific path, you must come up with a game plan. Even if it's going to change. Because there is no one route to success, it's so very easy to become overwhelmed by choices and again, have no idea what to do.

When I feel stuck these are the questions I ask myself to hone in on a game plan and next steps:

- How can I improve my craft?
- Are my marketing materials as strong as they can possibly be?
- How can I create genuine relationships with decision-makers in the industry?

- How can I add value to people who might be able to move my career forward?
- Am I constantly reminding my network and the industry that I'm alive?
- What am I most excited about spending time on right now?

Ask yourself those questions, use this book, hire a business coach, interview people who've achieved what you think you want. Establish some possible steps you can take and methods to approach your goals. Start with the end in mind and work backwards. But no matter what, do something.

It's my experience that we are very unlikely to make progress or create clarity by sitting on our couch thinking about what we're going to do. It's only by jumping into life with two feet that these things reveal themselves. You can read Stanislavsky all you want, but nothing compares to stepping onto stage in front of an audience.

Lesson 4: One small step every day adds up

The good news is that seemingly tiny steps really do turn into extraordinary results over time. The human mind overestimates what it can accomplish in a short period of time—I can totally get these 18 things done today!—and underestimates what it can accomplish over a long period of time. Think back to how different your entire life was 10 years ago.

You don't need to make your entire career happen today. You don't need to get an agent today. You don't need to create your demo reel today. Your job is to pick the simplest, next immediate action and merely do that one thing. And then the next thing. Then the next. (Pro tip: Bring joy to all that you do!)

There's an added benefit: action cures fear. So often we convince ourselves that once we're no longer afraid, once we have the confidence—then we'll take action. I've discovered it's the other way around. Take the leap. Make that scary phone call. Attend the intimidating event. It's only through action that fear dissipates.

Lesson 5: Enjoy the journey

Even if you win an Oscar, that evening will only be a few hours of your life. If you aren't loving the vast majority of the time leading up to—and after—those couple of hours then it's time to either change what you're doing, or transform your relationship to what you're doing.

On a somber note, reflect on how many incredible celebrities have committed suicide. All the money and accolades and fame in the world will not bring genuine happiness. I'm not saying every day will be rainbows and unicorns, but you were given this life to enjoy it. To soak up all the deliciousness of human connection. To make a difference in other people's lives, take part in telling incredible stories, and leave the world a better place than you found it.

So what do you do at 9am on a random Tuesday? The choice is yours ...

Jordan Ancel, Writer, Producer, Director

Jordan Ancel is an award-winning writer and director, serial entrepreneur, author, and artist with strong leadership skills and a commitment to inspiring success in others by providing CEOs, entrepreneurs, and artists with his unique brand of coaching and problem-solving. With over 20 years of experience in the entertainment industry, startups, internet advertising, marketing, and branding, his profound understanding of these industries gives him the tools to conceive and execute high-concept ideas with great success. For more information on Jordan, visit www.thrivingactor.com.

Leveling up your career

The following is excerpted from the forthcoming book *Thriving Actor: Go From Barely Surviving To Working and Thriving Right Now!* by Jordan Ancel.

As a filmmaker/producer and career coach for artists, I firmly believe that if actors run their careers like businesspeople, they will go farther faster. With this comes the one thing all businesses must do: market their product to the right audience so they can sell more of it. Specifically, as an actor, you need to market amazing, memorable performances in meaty roles that make people pause and take notice of you.

Almost all actors are doing it wrong. In an effort to get more opportunities, they purchase new headshots (they think their current ones "aren't working"), take more acting classes, and do more casting-director workshops. When they see no improvement, they rinse and repeat with different photographers, coaches, and workshops. Their bank accounts dwindle, and before they know it, they're the cliché of "broke actor."

They are the living definition of insanity: repeating the same ineffective behavior over and over again expecting different and better results ... while going broke! And all of this is just to build a list of Co-Star and Guest Star credits of only one or two lines each, which don't even pay them back what they put out. Insanity.

Imagine that you could have the perfect starring role, a meaty one, that shows off your acting chops and makes people actually see what you can do. How do you get those perfect starring roles? YOU CREATE THEM!

Add up all the money you spent this year on headshots, classes, coaches, seminars, workshops, and shooting fake scenes to look like you were in something. Next year, use that money to create a short film or web series that you can star in—that you can shine in. Use that to show your audience of industry and fans what you can really do. Give them the full you, not some broken pieces scattered across a reel that few will watch all the way through.

This is the point where most actors' fear kicks in, followed by all the excuses. "I'm not a writer," "I don't know where to begin," "I don't have the money," and "I can't ask people for money." Ok. You don't have to do everything yourself. Collaborate with people who are writers, directors, and budding producers. Just look through your Facebook or Instagram—surely you know at least one of these people, and they surely know others.

Creating and producing a starring vehicle is essential in order to level up your career.

1 It changes the conversation with industry people! You go from an actor needing a job to a producer creating your own work, which is always impressive. It shows you've got hustle. It shows that you're committed to your dreams no matter what. People don't see you as someone who's just waiting for a break, they see you as someone who has drive, passion, and guts. Instead of "Please hire me," you can say, "Check out this killer project I've created."

2 Film Festivals. When you have a project in a film festival, you have the potential to win awards. Those count for something. Especially in the more prestigious festivals, should you get in. Plus, just getting into festivals is a huge accomplishment. You also can create buzz for your project and yourself.

3 Agents, managers, CDs, and everyone can see you actually acting. Again, saying a few lines in a few shows or films is great when you can get them, but starring in something with an emotional arc allows everyone to see how good you are.

4 If you do have an agent and/or manager, it gives them something to market! They can't pitch for roles if you've got nothing substantial to show. It makes their job easier when you have a role you stand out in.

5 It alleviates the stress and angst and feelings of being idle. When you're working on something that you're passionate about, you won't feel like you're not accomplishing anything—you'll be accomplishing something huge. You'll also be less nervous about auditions because

you know you are already starring in something. That levity in your mood and demeanor, and that relaxation will actually improve your auditions!

Plus, creating and starring in your own project will absolutely lead to other opportunities by creating a whole bunch of new relationships with people, including crew, filmmakers, actors, and writers, who are also connecting to industry people outside of your circle.

And, perhaps most important, you'll feel more fulfilled having done something you love.

Howard Fine, Acting Coach, Howard Fine Acting Studio

During his 30-year teaching career, Howard Fine has been a celebrity acting coach for Hollywood stars. His classes are sought after by agents and managers for their clients and by actors of all levels who are looking to sustain a successful career in the industry.

Criteria for the professional actor

Wendy: When an actor first starts working with you, what are some of the habits or "default settings" that you look to disrupt or challenge? What is at the core of your approach?

Howard: The biggest misconception about acting is the idea of playing a character. Think of how many roles we play throughout the course of a day, and they are all parts of us. Learning to use yourself authentically is the key. If an actor has acquired life habits that interfere with their ability to communicate effectively these habits must be addressed. I recommend that every actor study the Alexander Technique in order to rid themselves of unconscious and unwanted physical habits. The study of voice is also an essential part of training. The actor must learn how to use their instrument properly. An actor must have a mind, body, and soul capable of connecting to anything that a writer has created. Great actors are also avid readers. You cannot expect to understand scripts if you don't read. Some people chose an acting career because they were bad academically and think that acting will be an easy option. Unfortunately for them, they soon discover that acting will call upon every skill that they failed to develop. The best actors make it look easy and yet it is extremely difficult to do at the highest level.

W: What are the elements that an actor can expect in a class setting? Why is a class setting the best place to start?

H: Acting is a contact sport. It must be done with other people. I can coach someone through a role in a one-on-one setting, but training can only take place in a class. You must have the opportunity to watch others make mistakes and solve problems they are also experiencing. Often the breakthrough happens when you watch someone else put it together and you understand how it applies to you. Everyone should start in a technique class. I have had some people take a professional level audition class as their first experience. They are trying to learn to book jobs that they are not qualified to do. Class should take you on a journey and provide you with the tools of the craft. There are two extremes to avoid when selecting a coach. There are coaches who are angry and cruel in their critiques. This will shut most artists down and make them afraid to make a mistake. Mistakes are part of learning, and we cannot grow if we don't make them. The other extreme is the coach who compliments everything and acts as a cheerleader. You cannot grow without criticism.

W: How does an actor identify material that fits who they are?

H: I would advise actors to try a wide range of material at first before trying to identify what they do best. You might discover that you are adept at physical comedy or that period work is your passion. Don't try to specialize at first. Over time you should develop a sense of what you are good at. Look at roles that have already been cast and start to think about what you feel you could have played. I think that it is very helpful to consult with industry professionals in order to get a sense of where you fit in the profession.

W: Is there ever a kind of material you would coach an actor to stay away from?

H: This is a question that every actor has to answer for themselves based on their own ethical and moral compass. I have students who have refused to do slasher films as they cannot abide the disregard for human life. I certainly would advise against doing pornography. There are extremes however which can make this profession a poor fit. I have come across certain potential actors who won't say what they consider bad words/foul language, and in that case they are going to take themselves out of the running for the majority of projects.

W: If actors want to work on very specific material like superhero types or broad comedy, what advice would you give them? How often do actors work on their own written material?

H: I offer classes where we tackle extremes such as superhero/villain. It is still about authentic use of the self, but the stakes tend to be very high. In all of these characters there must be vulnerability. Superman would not be interesting without Kryptonite. I want to see actors take other peoples words and *make* them their own, so I only allow scenes from published material. But I do have a student who is a best selling author, and in his case he gets to do some of his own writing.

W: How often do you find actors that are stuck in a choice or unable to risk making changes? How do you deal with that? What if they can't do what you are trying to help with?

H: I have come across actors who will not raise their voices above a low volume. They are scared of being too much. That actor is frightened of fully expressing themselves and must learn full investment. The other end of the spectrum are actors who constantly push and are overly broad. That actor is frightened of being boring. They must learn to be simple and real. These issues are very hard to resolve because they are connected to life issues. What stops you in your life, stops you in your work. I advise professional counseling to deal with these issues. There are actors who have such serious control issues that they will not let go and live in the moment. I had someone say "I thought my control issues were under control." He wasn't joking when he said it but quickly realized how funny the statement is. Again these are life issues that interfere with an actor's ability to do the work. They must be solved before the acting teacher can do his/her job.

W: How do you manage giving feedback? In class vs privately? Do students benefit more from hearing feedback in one-on-one coaching?

H: When a scene or exercise is over I ask, "What worked, what didn't and why?" I teach my students to self-evaluate before I say anything. This helps actors become self-sufficient artists. The fact that "What worked?" is a question creates balance. In order to gain confidence, the actor must know what they did well so that they can build on it. Because the actor joins me in the critique it helps take the sting out of the criticism. I teach my students that we are discussing technique, not talent. Their talent doesn't come and go because they made mistakes. When I coach privately, which is only for professional auditions or roles that the actor has already booked, I help more than I do in class. In class I will let the actors struggle, giving them just enough to hopefully discover the answers for themselves. If the teacher directs, they rob the actor of discovery.

W: When do you know an actor has had a breakthrough? When does the actor know? Does it happen at the same time?

H: The best part of teaching is watching actors put it all together. Breakthroughs are individual and are based on the specific challenges that the artist is facing. We usually all realize it at the same time. I do not encourage competition among actors. I tell my students that their only competition is with themselves to do their best work. Because of this, I have seen classmates moved to tears during special moments when a colleague is on fire with the work. This is incredibly rewarding and lifts everyone.

W: How important is it for actors to understand the genre and tone of the piece they are working on?

H: This goes to the issue of being an avid reader. You cannot expect to do anything without having a context with which to understand. In terms of having a career that lasts, it is essential to be able to play a wide variety of roles from different periods. You also must be able to tell the difference between a romantic comedy and a procedural drama. My students ask me all of the time how they can get better at script analysis. I advise everyone to write a two to three page scene as an exercise. They quickly realize that nothing is there by accident. They will agonize over time, place, relationship, and dialogue and hopefully get more in tune with what a writer has given them.

W: How important is it for you to like your students? What are the prerequisites/criteria for studying at your studio?

H: The issue of likeability is very important to success. A friend of mine who is very accomplished said that, "You succeed in business because others want you to succeed." This is invaluable advice. Some people have a chip on their shoulder, and they don't realize that no one will want to work with them as a result. I won't work with someone who is defensive or lazy. It is not fair to the majority of students who want to learn. A difficult personality can drain the teacher and the class. Anyone can sign up for our technique class initially, but not all actors complete the course or are invited to continue afterward. The class *is* the audition for the studio. In the six weeks of technique, we assess work ethic and attitude. You must be invited to continue after that, and further cuts are made as we go.

W: You have created a program and have been working for years with young artists in Melbourne, Australia. How are the Australian actors you work with different from American actors? Do they have the same set of expectations coming into class? What challenges/advantages are unique to that demographic?

H: I've often joked that there must be something in the water in Australia that creates so much acting talent. I think because they don't have Hollywood as part of the culture, the majority of those pursuing an acting career are doing it for the right reasons. They truly love the craft and do not have stars in their eyes. Sadly, there is a ton of talent and not nearly enough work to go around. I have found the actors in Australia to be very dedicated and to have a terrific work ethic.

Further Reading

Bialy, Sharon (2016), *How to Audition on Camera: A Hollywood Insider's Guide for Actors*: Tilbury House Publishers.

Dweck, Carol S. (2007), Mindset: *The New Psychology of Success*: Ballantine Books.

Edwards, Kelly (2017), *The Executive Chair*: HarperCollins Leadership.

Fine, Howard with Chris Freeman (2009), *Fine on Acting*: Havenhurst Books.

Gilbert, Daniel (2007), *Stumbling on Happiness*: Vintage Books.

Miller, Donald (2007), *Building a StoryBrand: Clarify Your Message So Customers Will Listen*: HarperCollins Leadership.

Morin, Amy (2014), *13 Things Mentally Strong People Don't Do*: William Morrow.

Pressfield, Steven (2011), *War of Art*: Black Irish Entertainment LLC.

Rilke, Rainer Maria (2011), *Letters to a Young Poet*. First published 1929 and translated by Charlie Louth from *Letters to a Young Poet & The Letter from the Young Worker*: Penguin Classics.

Seligman, Martin E. P. (2006), *Learned Optimism – How to Change Your Mind and Your Life*: Vintage Books/Division of Random House, Inc.

Selkowe, Rebecca Eve (2016), *Dominate the Debt*: Vivace Media LLC.

Stutz, Phil and Barry Michels (2012), *The Tools—5 Tools to Help You Find Courage, Creativity, and Willpower—and Inspire You to Live Life in Forward Motion*: Simon and Schuster.

Tharp, Twyla (2003), *The Creative Habit—Learn It and Use It for Life*: Simon and Schuster.

Acknowledgments

I want to start out by saying that writing a book is probably the most difficult endeavor I have ever taken on! I have an even deeper understanding and respect for writers. The discipline alone was at a new level. If a global pandemic hadn't sequestered me at home, I , like many creatives, would have struggled to stay on task. Every time I was tired, frustrated, tapped out of ideas and words to articulate my vision I would look for any distraction I could think of. I have never gone to the refrigerator so much in my life!

First and foremost, I want to thank two exceptional people who helped me articulate my ideas and challenged me to expand my conversation and thoughts in the most accessible way possible. Jane Borden and Isabel Wynne, you both pushed me forward throughout the writing process. Each of you gave me your creative time and input in countless ways. I am forever grateful.

To the colleagues who contributed to the "Industry Voices" section. Michael, Carol, Lisa, Candido, Cassandra, Nikki, Marci, Jonathan, Jordan, Ben, and Howard. I am honored to include these esteemed professionals. I would also like to acknowledge both Rebecca Selkowe and Miata Edoga, who have shared countless hours educating me and young artists alike to the financial realities of a creative career.

To the professionals who wrote me the most glorious testimonials endorsing my work: David, Sharon, Seth, Leslie, Harry, Iris, Ro, Tim, Grant, Jennifer, and John. Every one of you supported me with your thoughtfulness and willingness to contribute.

To the many artists/actors who contributed their stories to my book: Emma Jean, Jordan Hudec, Isabella Oliveri, Isabel Wynne, Rae'l Ba and Bianca Beach. I am grateful to have been your teacher and mentor and I am inspired by the dedication and talent you all bring to your creative journeys.

To my colleagues in academia: Luke Yankee, Grant Kretchik, Jorge Cachiero, John Benitz, Tamiko Washington, Cosmin Chivu, Brian Kite, Harry Winer, Dolann Adams, and Jennifer Holmes. Thank you for your support, guidance, and the access to the most wonderful students.

To my fellow Casting Society Board members and community. I am proud to be a part of the leadership.

Thank you to all the industry professionals who have shared their time and expertise at the Pace Intensive I co-created in 2014 and which is still going strong. Throughout the years the list has expanded to include a wide representation of our industry. Thankfully, too numerous to list . . . you know who you are and how much I appreciate you.

To my personal support group: David Auerbach, who's infinite confidence was a blessing every day. He has taught me the value of flushing out my ideas to their fullest, being concise and has supported me no matter what I needed to grow as a professional. My three children: Bryan, Ethan, and Lauren. Each in their own way keep me focused, honest, and wanting to inspire. They push me to better and help me see the world through their lenses. My sister, Leslie, who has always made my questions and struggles a priority. She has lovingly given me feedback and help throughout all of my personal and professional endeavors. My parents, Evey and Larry, who have always encouraged me to ask questions and make my own way in this world.

To Reuben Cannon, Joel Thurm, and Keli Lee who were my most formative and beloved bosses and who helped shape me as a professional.

And a world of thanks to both Judy Polone and Robert Greenwald who made casting a dream profession for me. The trust, and autonomy you gave me to develop my voice and shine will never be forgotten. Working for producers like you spoiled me forever.

Index